Programming Sudoku

Wei-Meng Lee

Apress®

Programming Sudoku

Copyright © 2006 by Wei-Meng Lee

ISBN-13 (pbk): 978-1-59059-662-3

ISBN-10 (pbk): 1-59059-662-5

Printed and bound in the United States of America 9 8 7 6 5 4 3 2 1

Lead Editor: Dominic Shakeshaft
Technical Reviewer: Andy Olsen
Editorial Board: Steve Anglin, Dan Appleman, Ewan Buckingham, Gary Cornell, Jason Gilmore, Jonathan Hassell, James Huddleston, Chris Mills, Matthew Moodie, Dominic Shakeshaft, Jim Sumser, Keir Thomas, Matt Wade
Project Manager and Production Director: Grace Wong
Copy Edit Manager: Nicole LeClerc
Copy Editor: Bill McManus
Assistant Production Director: Kari Brooks-Copony
Production Editor: Katie Stence
Compositor: Susan Glinert
Proofreader: Lori Bring
Indexer: Carol Burbo
Artist: April Milne
Cover Designer: Kurt Krames
Manufacturing Director: Tom Debolski

Distributed to the book trade worldwide by Springer-Verlag New York, Inc., 233 Spring Street, 6th Floor, New York, NY 10013. Phone 1-800-SPRINGER, fax 201-348-4505, e-mail orders-ny@springer-sbm.com, or visit http://www.springeronline.com.

For information on translations, please contact Apress directly at 2560 Ninth Street, Suite 219, Berkeley, CA 94710. Phone 510-549-5930, fax 510-549-5939, e-mail info@apress.com, or visit http://www.apress.com.

The source code for this book is available to readers at http://www.apress.com in the Source Code section. You will need to answer questions pertaining to this book in order to successfully download the code.

Contents at a Glance

Contents

About the Author

WEI-MENG LEE is a technologist and founder of Developer Learning Solutions, a technology company that specializes in hands-on training in the latest Microsoft technologies. Wei-Meng speaks regularly at international conferences and has authored and coauthored numerous books on .NET, XML, and wireless technologies, including *ASP.NET 2.0: A Developer's Notebook* and *Visual Basic 2005 Jumpstart* (both from O'Reilly Media). He is also the coauthor of the Apress title *XML Programming Using the Microsoft XML Parser.*
Find out about the latest books and articles by Wei-Meng at his blog: `http://weimenglee.blogspot.com/`.

About the Technical Reviewer

ANDY OLSEN is a freelance developer, instructor, and writer based in Swansea in Wales. Andy has been using Microsoft technologies for 20 years, back in the days when the words "Visual Basic" were a contradiction in terms. Andy would like to thank his wife Jayne for her patience against all the odds, and Emily and Thomas for all the fun. Cymru am Byth!

Acknowledgments

The initial idea for this book started when I was browsing at a local bookstore. Looking at the mountain of Sudoku books piled up at one prominent spot of the bookstore, I wondered what the craze was all about. After picking one up to have a quick glance, I finally understood: Sudoku puzzles not only are fun and challenging to solve, they offer good training for thinking logically. That inspired me to write a program to solve Sudoku puzzles programmatically, and then to write this book.

While most publishers are only interested in publishing Sudoku puzzles book, Gary Cornell had the faith in me to say "yes" when I proposed doing a book on Sudoku programming. For that, I am grateful to Gary and I hope that I have not disappointed him. Thank you, Gary!

I also want to express my sincere gratitude to my editor, Dominic Shakeshaft, whose editing skill has definitely made this book a better read, and to my technical reviewer, Andy Olsen, who has studiously checked every line of code that I have written—I am forever amazed by his laser-sharp accuracy. Dominic and Andy are the best combination that a publisher could ever offer to an author. I wish I could work with them on my next book! Thank you, Dominic and Andy!

Thanks are also due to the early beta testers of my Sudoku puzzles—Jon Wright, Adam Mozdzynski, Cynthia N. Vance, and Robert Douglas. I am grateful for your time and your willingness to share your Soduku experiences with me.

Not forgetting the heroes behind the scenes, I want to thank Grace Wong for her great management of this project, Bill McManus for reading and editing my writing to make sure that readers will be able to enjoy the book, Katie Stence for her great work in getting the book ready for production, and last but not least, Tina Nielsen for making all the necessary arrangements to get this project going.

Introduction

Sudoku is the wildly popular new puzzle game that is taking the world by storm. Sudoku puzzles are 9×9 grids, and each square in the grid consists of a 3×3 subgrid called a minigrid. Your goal is to fill in the squares so that each column, row, and minigrid contains the numbers 1 through 9 exactly once. And some squares already contain numbers or symbols, which lend clues toward the solution. While the rules of Sudoku are extremely simple, solving a Sudoku puzzle is an intellectual challenge.

What This Book Covers

Programming Sudoku provides you with great approaches to building and solving Sudoku puzzles. Using logical deduction and analysis, you'll learn how to get a computer to solve these puzzles for you. You will learn the various techniques that you can deploy to solve a puzzle, ranging from basic techniques such as Column, Row, and Minigrid Elimination, to the more advanced triplets identification technique. And if all logical techniques fail, brute-force elimination will kick into action and solve the puzzle by making some educated guesses. In addition to solving Sudoku puzzles, you will also learn the techniques for programmatically generating Sudoku puzzles of varying levels of difficulty.

One of the myths about Sudoku is that you must be good in mathematics to play the game. The fact is that people of all ages can enjoy Sudoku, regardless of whether they are mathematically inclined. All you need is a logical mind and a great amount of patience. I will teach you how to logically deduce a number for a cell and how one confirmed cell can lead to the confirmation of other cells in the grid. Even if you are not a programmer, this book will provide you with a better understanding of how to logically solve a Sudoku puzzle.

While the code project provided in this book uses the Visual Basic 2005 programming language, C# programmers should not have any major problem understanding or translating the code. This book should be a fun, intriguing read whether you're a novice or advanced programmer. You'll find this book interesting whatever your programming background. The core techniques in the book enable you to solve Sudoku on any programming platform.

The following sections provide an overview of this book.

Chapter 1 – What Is Sudoku?

This chapter introduces you to Sudoku and explains the basics of how to play the game. You will also walk through a scaled-down version of a Sudoku puzzle to understand how the puzzle is solved step by step.

Chapter 2 – Creating the Sudoku Application

In this chapter, you will walk through the various steps to construct a Sudoku puzzle board using a Windows application. This is the foundation chapter that all future chapters will build on. Although the application in this chapter lacks the intelligence required to solve a Sudoku puzzle, it does allow you to play Sudoku on the computer. Moreover, the application that you build in this chapter provides some aid to beginning Sudoku players, because it checks for compliance with the rules of Sudoku.

Chapter 3 – Basic Sudoku Solving Technique

In this chapter, you will learn how a Sudoku puzzle can be solved by using the elimination technique, named Column, Row, and Minigrid Elimination (CRME). While the CRME technique has its limitations, it nevertheless is able to solve many simple Sudoku puzzles.

Chapter 4 – Intermediate Techniques

In this chapter, you will learn about the lone ranger technique and how it is useful in helping you to solve or weaken some difficult Sudoku puzzles. Lone rangers are extremely useful and can always help to directly solve a Sudoku puzzle.

Chapter 5 – Advanced Techniques

In this chapter, you will learn the three advanced techniques that you can use to solve Sudoku puzzles: twins, triplets, and brute-force elimination. Although most of the time the twins and triplets techniques will not directly solve the puzzle, they are good techniques for "softening" the puzzle so that the puzzle can be solved by other techniques such as CRME and lone rangers. You will also learn how to use the brute-force technique to make an educated guess when all the other techniques have failed.

Chapter 6 – Generating Sudoku Puzzles

This chapter combines all the techniques that you have learned in the past few chapters and uses them to generate Sudoku puzzles of varying levels of difficulty. While I will describe the techniques to generate Sudoku puzzles, you can adapt the methods to further improve the quality of the puzzles. In fact, there are many areas of improvement that you might want to look into, such as adjusting the weights assigned to each technique that is used to solve a puzzle to further fine-tune the difficulty levels. Also, you can insert additional checks in the program so that the puzzles generated can have only one solution.

Chapter 7 – How to Play Kakuro

In this chapter, you will learn how to play the new Kakuro puzzle game. If you are coming from a Sudoku background, you should not find the puzzle too difficult.

Obtaining This Book's Source Code

The source code for this book can be obtained from http://apress.com/book/download.html. To run the code, you need Microsoft Visual Studio 2005.

CHAPTER 1

■ ■ ■

What Is Sudoku?

Sudoku is a puzzle game that is taking the world by storm. The name *Sudoku* comes from the Japanese word (shown in Figure 1-1) that means "number place." The first Sudoku puzzle was published in the United States, but Sudoku initially became popular in Japan, in 1986, and did not attain international popularity until 2005.

数独

Figure 1-1. *The word Sudoku in Japanese*

The rules of Sudoku are extremely simple, yet solving a Sudoku puzzle is an intellectual challenge. A Sudoku puzzle contains a 9×9 grid, which is divided into nine smaller 3×3 grids (known as minigrids). Figure 1-2 shows a Sudoku grid with its nine minigrids.

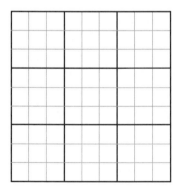

Figure 1-2. *A Sudoku grid*

Rules of Sudoku

The aim of the game is to place a number from 1 to 9 into each of the cells, such that each number must appear exactly once in each row and in each column in the grid. Additionally, each minigrid must contain all the numbers 1 through 9. It's also possible to use any other set of symbols. However, using numbers is the obvious choice.

Figure 1-3 shows a partially completed Sudoku grid with the first row and column completed and the first minigrid completed.

7	4	6	2	9	1	5	8	3
8	5	2						
9	1	3						
1								
6								
5								
2								
3								
4								

Figure 1-3. *A partially completed Sudoku puzzle*

A Sudoku puzzle usually comes with a partially filled grid. The aim is to complete the grid in the shortest amount of time. Figure 1-4 shows a partially filled grid at the start of a Sudoku puzzle.

		9		5			6	
3		2	1	9			8	7
	6		3					
		8	5		3			1
1	7						5	4
5			8		1	2		
				7		2		
4	8			1	2	5		3
	2			3		7		

Figure 1-4. *A Sudoku puzzle*

At first glance, a Sudoku puzzle looks simple enough, but upon further examination, it is not as trivial as you might have initially imagined. The placement of the various numbers in a partially filled Sudoku puzzle determines the level of difficulty of the game.

LEVELS OF DIFFICULTY

There are no hard and fast rules that dictate the difficulty level of a Sudoku puzzle. A sparsely filled Sudoku puzzle may be extremely easy to solve, whereas a densely filled Sudoku puzzle may actually be more difficult to solve. In Chapter 6, I will discuss how a Sudoku puzzle can be graded based on the techniques used to solve it.

From a mathematical perspective, it has been proven that the total number of valid Sudoku grids is 6,670,903,752,021,072,936,960 (that's why you will never run out of puzzles to solve!).

■**Note** If you are interested in how this magical number was derived, check out the paper from Bertram Felgenhauer and Frazer Jarvis detailing the methodology of their analysis at `http://www.shef.ac.uk/~pm1afj/sudoku/`.

Solving a Sudoku puzzle requires patience and a lot of logical thinking. Sometimes a Sudoku puzzle has more than one solution. From a computing perspective, using brute force seems to be the most direct way to solve a Sudoku puzzle. A combination of recursion and backtracking guarantees that a solution will ultimately be derived (if a puzzle is solvable in the first place). However, due to the large number of combinations available, using brute force is always the last resort. In fact, most Sudoku puzzles can be solved by the logical method of deduction. I will give you an example of this in the upcoming section "It's Just Logic!"

Sudoku Terminology

A Sudoku puzzle usually contains nine columns and nine rows. Within this 9×9 grid are nine minigrids. In Figure 1-5, I have labeled each minigrid from 1 to 9, with minigrid 1 at the top-left corner and minigrid 9 at the bottom-right corner.

Throughout this book, I will refer to each cell in the grid by its column number followed by its row number. Figure 1-6 shows the coordinates of each cell in the grid.

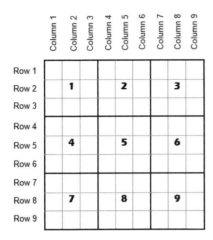

Figure 1-5. *The rows and columns in a Sudoku puzzle*

(1,1)	(2,1)	(3,1)	(4,1)	(5,1)	(6,1)	(7,1)	(8,1)	(9,1)
(1,2)	(2,2)	(3,2)	(4,2)	(5,2)	(6,2)	(7,2)	(8,2)	(9,2)
(1,3)	(2,3)	(3,3)	(4,3)	(5,3)	(6,3)	(7,3)	(8,3)	(9,3)
(1,4)	(2,4)	(3,4)	(4,4)	(5,4)	(6,4)	(7,4)	(8,4)	(9,4)
(1,5)	(2,5)	(3,5)	(4,5)	(5,5)	(6,5)	(7,5)	(8,5)	(9,5)
(1,6)	(2,6)	(3,6)	(4,6)	(5,6)	(6,6)	(7,6)	(8,6)	(9,6)
(1,7)	(2,7)	(3,7)	(4,7)	(5,7)	(6,7)	(7,7)	(8,7)	(9,7)
(1,8)	(2,8)	(3,8)	(4,8)	(5,8)	(6,8)	(7,8)	(8,8)	(9,8)
(1,9)	(2,9)	(3,9)	(4,9)	(5,9)	(6,9)	(7,9)	(8,9)	(9,9)

Figure 1-6. *The coordinates of cells in a Sudoku grid*

It's Just Logic!

Most Sudoku puzzles can actually be solved by applying some simple logic. As an example, let's consider the Sudoku puzzle shown in Figure 1-7, originally published in the *Chicago Sun-Times* on November 8, 2005.

	3	4				9		
6				8	2	1	4	
		1		2	7			
4		9		8	3		5	
5	6					8	7	
	2		5	6		4		1
			2	1		8		
8	5	7	9					6
	9				3	4		

Figure 1-7. *A sample Sudoku puzzle*

In order to solve the puzzle, you have to start somewhere. Consider cell (7,4), shown with the circle in Figure 1-8. First scan through the row that it is in, followed by the column, and then finally within the minigrid itself. By scanning the row, you notice that the possible values for (7,4) are 1, 2, 6, and 7 (since 4, 9, 8, 3, and 5 are already in the row). However, when you then scan the column, you can immediately eliminate 2 as a possibility (since the column already contains 2), leaving only 1, 6, and 7 as possible values for cell (7,4). Finally, looking within the minigrid, you see that 1 and 7 are already present, so the only possible value for (7,4) is 6.

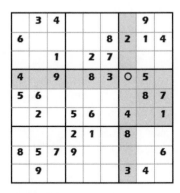

Figure 1-8. *Resolving the value for cell (7,4)*

So now you can confidently fill in (7,4) with 6, as shown in Figure 1-9.

	3	4					9	
6					8	2	1	4
		1		2	7			
4		9		8	3	6	5	
5	6						8	7
	2		5	6		4		1
			2	1		8		
8	5	7	9					6
	9					3	4	

Figure 1-9. *Filling in the value for cell (7,4)*

The next obvious cell to fill in is (9,4), because the row, column, and minigrid in which it exists already include most values between 1 and 9. Again, scanning the row, the possible values are 1, 2, and 7. Scanning by column leaves 2 as the only possible value. Since there is now only one possible value for (9,4), you can fill it in with 2, as shown in Figure 1-10, without even examining the minigrid.

	3	4					9	
6					8	2	1	4
		1		2	7			
4		9		8	3	6	5	2
5	6						8	7
	2		5	6		4		1
			2	1		8		
8	5	7	9					6
	9					3	4	

Figure 1-10. *Filling in the value for cell (9,4)*

As you can see, this process repeats itself. And as you fill in more and more cells, ultimately you will solve the puzzle. Besides using the elimination technique (which I have aptly given the name *Column, Row, and Minigrid Elimination*, or CRME; more on this in Chapter 2) that I showed in this section, there are some other, not-so-obvious techniques that you can use to solve a Sudoku puzzle. All of these techniques use logical deductions to derive a number for a cell. You will learn more about these techniques in subsequent chapters.

■**Note** While most puzzles can be solved by logic alone, there are indeed some difficult puzzles that require you to solve using the trial-and-error method.

Variants of Sudoku

Besides the standard 9×9 grid, variants of Sudoku puzzles include the following:

- 4×4 grid with 2×2 minigrids.

- 5×5 grid with pentomino (http://en.wikipedia.org/wiki/Pentomino) regions (published under the name Logi-5). A pentomino is composed of five congruent squares, connected orthogonally. If you have played the game Tetris before, you have seen a pentomino.

- 6×6 grid with 2×3 regions.

- 7×7 grid with six heptomino (http://mathworld.wolfram.com/Heptomino.html) regions and a disjoint region.

- 16×16 grid (Super Sudoku).

- 25×25 grid (Sudoku the Giant).

- A 3-D Sudoku puzzle (http://www.sudoku.org.uk/PDF/Dion_Cube.pdf) invented by Dion Church was published in the *Daily Telegraph* (in the U.K.) in May 2005.

- Alphabetical variations, which use letters rather than numbers. The *Guardian* (in the U.K.) calls these Godoku while others refer to them as Wordoku (see Figure 1-11).

■**Tip** For a detailed description of Sudoku variants, visit http://en.wikipedia.org/wiki/ Sudoku#Variants. *Wikipedia*, the free encyclopedia, has a good discussion of Sudoku at http://en. wikipedia.org/wiki/Sudoku.

A	B	C	D	E	F	G	H	I
D	F	G						
E	H	I						
F								
G								
H								
I								
B								
C								

Figure 1-11. *A sample Wordoku puzzle*

Let's Play Sudoku!

In the interest of space, let's work through a scaled-down 4×4 Sudoku puzzle from start to finish. The rules and techniques for a scaled-down Sudoku puzzle are the same as for a full-sized Sudoku puzzle, but the smaller size enables us to work through the solution from beginning to end much more quickly and easily, because fewer permutations are available. We will use the numbers 1 to 4 instead of 1 to 9, since there are now four cells in each row and column (as well as in each minigrid).

Consider the Sudoku puzzle shown in Figure 1-12.

1			3
	2		
	3		
2			4

Figure 1-12. *A 4×4 Sudoku puzzle*

The first cell that you can fill in is (2,4). After you scan both its row and column, you should get the value 1 (see Figure 1-13).

1			3
	2		
	3		
2	1		4

Figure 1-13. *Filling in the value for cell (2,4)*

The next logical cell is (3,4), which is value 3 (see Figure 1-14).

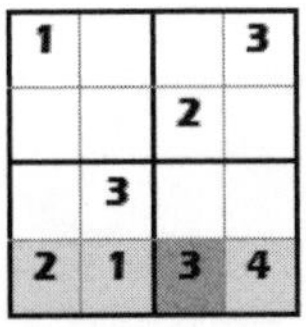

1			3
		2	
	3		
2	1	3	4

Figure 1-14. *Filling in the value for cell (3,4)*

And that leaves us with (1,3), which is value 4 (see Figure 1-15).

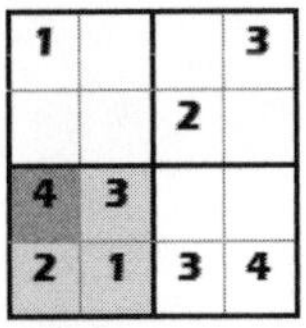

1			3
		2	
4	3		
2	1	3	4

Figure 1-15. *Filling in the value for cell (1,3)*

The next logical cell to fill in would be (1,2), which is value 3 (see Figure 1-16).

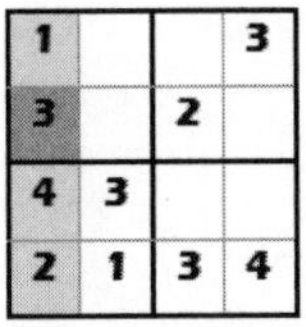

1			3
3		2	
4	3		
2	1	3	4

Figure 1-16. *Filling in the value for cell (1,2)*

That makes (4,2) a 1 (see Figure 1-17).

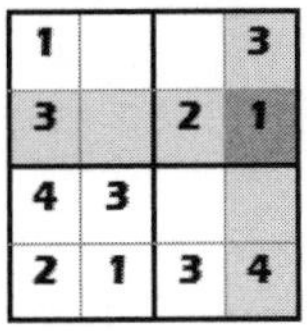

1			3
3		2	1
4	3		
2	1	3	4

Figure 1-17. *Filling in the value for cell (4,2)*

And, naturally, that makes cell (3,1) a 4 (see Figure 1-18).

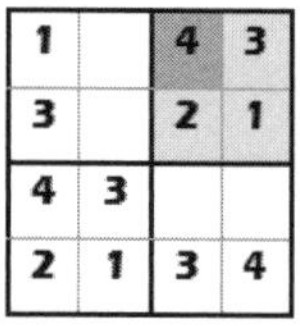

1		4	3
3		2	1
4	3		
2	1	3	4

Figure 1-18. *Filling in the value for cell (3,1)*

You can now easily fill in the rest of the blanks, as shown in Figure 1-19.

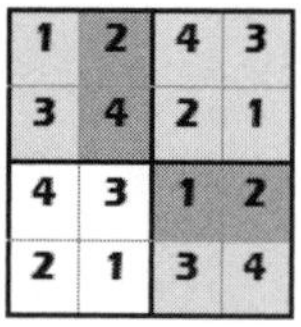

1	2	4	3
3	4	2	1
4	3	1	2
2	1	3	4

Figure 1-19. *Filling in the values for all remaining cells*

And that completes the puzzle!

USEFUL SUDOKU RESOURCES

Here are some useful resources on Sudoku:

- *Mathematics of Sudoku:* http://en.wikipedia.org/wiki/Mathematics_of_Sudoku

- *History of Sudoku:* http://en.wikipedia.org/wiki/Sudoku#History

- *Useful information on Sudoku:* http://www.answers.com/topic/sudoku

---

Summary

This chapter introduced you to Sudoku and explained the basics of how to play the game. You have also walked through a scaled-down version of a Sudoku puzzle. In the next chapter, you will start building your own Sudoku application. You will progressively add intelligence to it in the subsequent chapters so that you have a complete Sudoku solver.

CHAPTER 2

■ ■ ■

Creating the Sudoku Application

Now that you have a firm grounding in the basic rules of Sudoku, it is time for us to start the journey into solving Sudoku puzzles using computer programming. For this task, you will build a Windows application that represents a Sudoku puzzle. The application that you build in this chapter will act as a rule enforcer, helping you to make sure that a value inserted into a cell does not violate the rules of Sudoku. We aren't concerned about how to solve a Sudoku puzzle yet; we leave that for the next few chapters.

In this chapter, I walk you through the various steps to construct a Sudoku puzzle board using a Windows application. This is the foundation chapter that all future chapters will build on. While the application that you build in this chapter lacks the intelligence required to solve a Sudoku puzzle, it will provide you with many hours of entertainment. Moreover, it will provide some aid to beginning Sudoku players, because it helps to check for the rules of Sudoku. Your Sudoku application will have the capabilities to do the following:

- Load and save Sudoku puzzles

- Ensure that only valid numbers are allowed to be placed in a cell

- Check whether a Sudoku puzzle has been solved

- Keep track of the time needed to solve a Sudoku puzzle

- Undo and redo previous moves

As in all large software projects, I will be breaking the functionalities of the Sudoku application into various functions and subroutines. The following are the major tasks in this chapter:

- Creating the user interface of the Sudoku application

- Using arrays to represent values in the grid

- Storing the moves using the stack data structure

- Generating the grid dynamically using Label controls

- Handling click events on the Label controls

- Checking whether a move is valid

- Checking whether a puzzle is solved

- Updating the value of a cell

- Undoing and redoing a move

- Saving a game

- Opening a saved game

- Ending the game

At the end of this chapter, you will have a functional Sudoku application that you can use to solve your Sudoku puzzles!

Creating the Sudoku Project

The application that you will build in this chapter is a Windows application. Figure 2-1 shows how the application will look at the end of this chapter.

Using this application, users will be able to load and save puzzles to disk. The application will act as a rule enforcer, ensuring that the user cannot place a number in a cell that will violate the rules of Sudoku. This is useful for beginners who are learning Sudoku.

■**Note** The application in this chapter will not have the intelligence to solve a Sudoku puzzle yet. You will begin building the intelligence in Chapter 3.

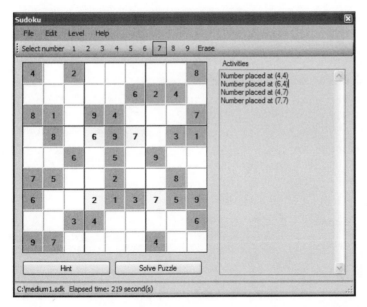

Figure 2-1. *The Sudoku application you will build in this chapter*

Creating the User Interface

For the Sudoku application, you will create a Windows application using Microsoft Visual Studio 2005. Launch Visual Studio 2005. Choose File ➤ New Project, select the Windows Application template, and name the project **Sudoku**.

■**Note** Throughout this book, I will use Visual Basic 2005 as the programming language. C# programmers should not have any major problem understanding/translating the code.

The project contains a default Windows form named Form1. Set the properties of Form1 as shown in Table 2-1. To change the property of a control in Visual Studio 2005, right-click the control and select Properties to open the Properties window.

Table 2-1. *Properties of Form1*

Property	Value
FormBorderStyle	FixedToolWindow
Size	551, 445
Text	Sudoku

Figure 2-2 shows how Form1 will look like after applying the properties listed in Table 2-1. Essentially, you are creating a fixed-size window.

Figure 2-2. *Modifying Form1*

Adding a MenuStrip Control

In the Toolbox, double-click the MenuStrip control located on the Menus & Toolbars tab to add a menu to Form1. In the MenuStrip Tasks menu (also known as a Smart Tag), click Insert Standard Items to insert a list of standard menu items.

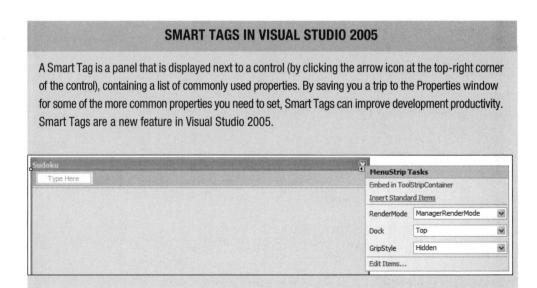

SMART TAGS IN VISUAL STUDIO 2005

A Smart Tag is a panel that is displayed next to a control (by clicking the arrow icon at the top-right corner of the control), containing a list of commonly used properties. By saving you a trip to the Properties window for some of the more common properties you need to set, Smart Tags can improve development productivity. Smart Tags are a new feature in Visual Studio 2005.

Once the standard menu items are inserted, you can customize the menu by removing menu items that are not relevant (use the Delete key to remove menu items) and inserting new items. Figure 2-3 shows the different menu items that you will add for this application.

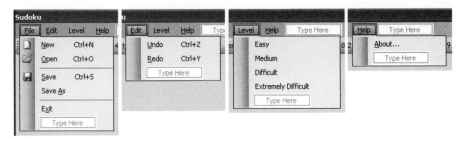

Figure 2-3. *The menu items for the Sudoku application*

■**Tip** The standard menus by default include a Tools menu rather than a Level menu. You can simply replace the Tools menu with the Level menu. In addition, you can change the menu items to Easy, Medium, Difficult, and Extremely Difficult. For the File, Edit, and Help menus, if you want to delete any menu items, simply select the unwanted item and press the Delete key.

To assign shortcuts to the different levels of difficulty, click each of the Level menu items and enter the values as shown in Table 2-2 (see also Figure 2-4).

Table 2-2. *Values to Set for the Level Menu and Its Menu Items*

Menu/Item	Value
Level	&Level
Easy	&Easy
Medium	&Medium
Difficult	&Difficult
Extremely Difficult	Ex&tremely Difficult

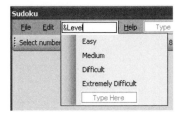

Figure 2-4. *Setting the values for the Level menu and its menu items*

After you set the values, the Level menu looks like Figure 2-5.

Figure 2-5. *The Level menu and its menu items*

Adding a ToolStrip Control

You will now add a ToolStrip control to the Windows form so that users can choose a number to insert into the cells. In the Toolbox, double-click the ToolStrip control (also located on the Menus & Toolbars tab) to add it onto Form1. You need to add Label and Button controls to the ToolStrip control; Figure 2-6 shows how to add controls to a ToolStrip control.

Figure 2-6. *Adding controls to the ToolStrip control*

Add a Label control to the ToolStrip control, and set the Text property of the Label control to **Select number.**

Next, add ten Button controls to the ToolStrip control. Set the DisplayStyle property of each Button control to Text. Set the Text property of the ten Button controls to **1, 2, 3, 4, 5, 6, 7, 8, 9,** and **Erase**, respectively, as shown in Figure 2-7, which depicts how the finished ToolStrip control should look.

Figure 2-7. *The finished ToolStrip control*

Adding a StatusStrip Control

You will also add to the bottom of the form a StatusStrip control (also located on the Menus & Toolbars tab). Click the StatusStrip control on the form and insert two StatusLabel controls (see Figure 2-8).

Figure 2-8. *Populating the StatusStrip control*

Figure 2-9 shows the form at this stage.

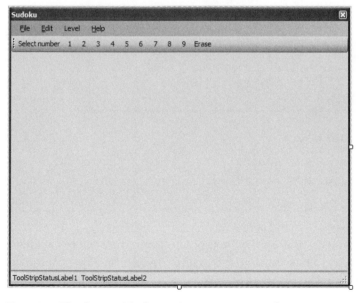

Figure 2-9. *The form with the various menu controls*

Adding Other Controls

The last step in creating the graphical user interface (GUI) of the Sudoku application is to add the various controls, as shown in Figure 2-10.

■**Note** What about drawing the Sudoku grid? Well, I will be using Label controls to represent the cells within a Sudoku grid. And since there are 81 of them, I will generate them dynamically. I will show you how to do this in the next section.

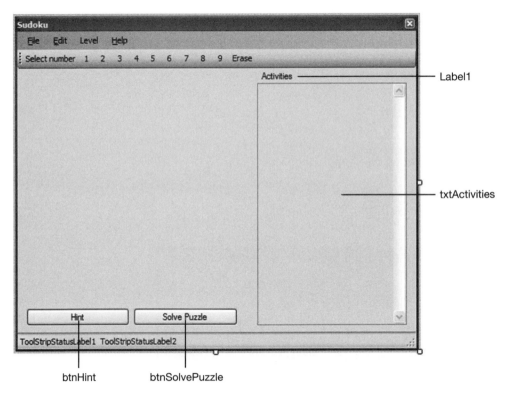

Figure 2-10. *Adding the various controls to Form1*

The txtActivities control is used to display the various moves played by the user. Set the properties of these controls as shown in Table 2-3.

Finally, add a Timer control (located on the Components tab in the Toolbox) to the form. Set its Interval property to 1000 (the unit is in milliseconds). The Timer control is used to keep track of the time taken to solve a Sudoku puzzle.

Table 2-3. *Properties of the Various Controls*

Control	Property	Value
Label (Label1)	Location	332, 53
Label (Label1)	Text	Activities
TextBox (txtActivities)	Location	329, 69
TextBox (txtActivities)	Multiline	True
TextBox (txtActivities)	Size	203, 321
TextBox (txtActivities)	Scrollbars	Vertical
Button (btnHint)	Text	Hint
Button (btnHint)	Location	12, 367
Button (btnHint)	Size	142, 23
Button (btnSolvePuzzle)	Text	Solve Puzzle
Button (btnSolvePuzzle)	Location	160, 367
Button (btnSolvePuzzle)	Size	142, 23

Declaring the Member Variables

Now that you have added the various controls to the form, it is time to switch to the code-behind of Form1 to add the various functionalities. In Solution Explorer, select Form1.vb and click the View Code button to switch to the code-behind of Form1 (see Figure 2-11).

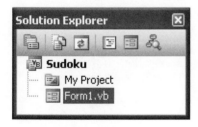

Figure 2-11. *Switching to code view*

In the Form1 class, add the following member variables (in bold):

```
Public Class Form1

    '---dimension of each cell in the grid---
    Const CellWidth As Integer = 32
    Const cellHeight As Integer = 32
```

```
'---offset from the top-left corner of the window---
Const xOffset As Integer = -20
Const yOffset As Integer = 25

'---color for empty cell---
Private DEFAULT_BACKCOLOR As Color = Color.White

'---color for original puzzle values---
Private FIXED_FORECOLOR As Color = Color.Blue
Private FIXED_BACKCOLOR As Color = Color.LightSteelBlue

'---color for user-inserted values---
Private USER_FORECOLOR As Color = Color.Black
Private USER_BACKCOLOR As Color = Color.LightYellow

'---the number currently selected for insertion---
Private SelectedNumber As Integer

'---stacks to keep track of all the moves---
Private Moves As Stack(Of String)
Private RedoMoves As Stack(Of String)

'---keep track of filename to save to---
Private saveFileName As String = String.Empty

'---used to represent the values in the grid---
Private actual(9, 9) As Integer

'---used to keep track of elapsed time---
Private seconds As Integer = 0

'---has the game started?---
Private GameStarted As Boolean = False
```

As you can see from the declaration, you first declared some constants to store the dimension of each cell in the Sudoku grid. You also declared some variables to store the various colors in the grid—all original values in the grid will have a blue background, while values placed by the user will have a yellow background. Empty cells have a white background.

Next, you declared two stack data structures—Moves and RedoMoves. A stack is a data structure that works on the last-in, first-out (LIFO) principle. This means that the last item pushed into a stack is the first item to be taken off. You use the Stack class to remember the moves you made so that if you need to undo the moves, you can do so. I will discuss this issue in more detail later in the chapter, in the section "Storing Moves in Stacks."

If you observe the declaration of the stack, you will notice that there is a new keyword, Of. This keyword is used when declaring a *generic* type. Support for generic types is a new feature in .NET Framework 2.0. In our case, the Stack class is a generic class. During declaration time, you use the Of keyword to indicate to the compiler that you can only push and pop string data types (and not other data types) into and from the Stack class. This helps to make your application safer and reduces the chance that you inadvertently push or pop the wrong types of data into the stack.

Representing Values in the Grid

A standard Sudoku puzzle consists of a grid of nine rows and nine columns, totaling 81 cells. A good way to represent a Sudoku grid is to use a two-dimensional array. As an example, the grid in Figure 2-12 will be represented in the array as follows (recall that a cell in a Sudoku puzzle is referenced by its column number followed by its row number):

```
actual(1,1) = 4
actual(2,1) = 0
actual(3,1) = 2
actual(4,1) = 0
actual(5,1) = 3
...
actual(1,2) = 7
...
```

Each empty cell in the grid is represented by the value 0.

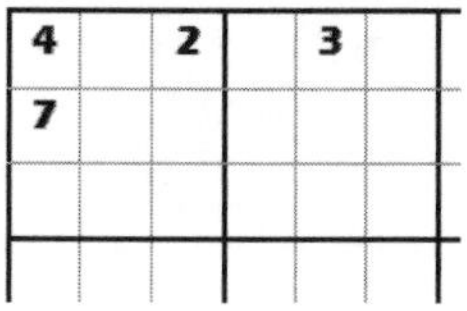

Figure 2-12. *Representing cells in a Sudoku grid using an array*

However, note that arrays in Visual Basic 2005 are zero-based. That is, when you declare the actual variable to be actual(9,9), there are actually 100 elements in it, from actual(0,0) to actual(9,9). For our application, the elements in row 0 and column 0 are left unused, as shown in Figure 2-13.

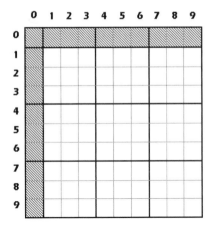

Figure 2-13. *Unused cells (shaded) in the array*

Naming Cells

Each cell in the grid will be represented using a dynamically generated Label control. You will need to assign a name to each Label control so that individual cells can be identified. For simplicity, in our application each cell will be identified based on its column and row numbers. For example, the Label control representing cell (1,1) will be named 11, cell (2,1) will be named 21, and so on.

Erasability of a Cell

A cell may contain a value set by the user or set originally as part of the puzzle. If the value is set by the user, it can be erased so that other values can be assigned to it. As such, there must be a way to identify if a particular cell value can be erased. For this purpose, you can use the Tag property of the Label control. As an example, if the value in cell (4,5) can be erased, you will set its Tag property to 1. If its value cannot be erased, then its Tag property would be 0.

Storing Moves in Stacks

To allow the user to undo and redo his moves, every time a number is placed in a cell, its coordinates and values are placed in a stack. When the user undoes his move, a value is popped from the stack and pushed into another stack. The value pushed into the stack is a three-digit string. For example, 349 means that cell (3,4) has been assigned the value 9. Figure 2-14 shows that when a user undoes a move, the value from the Moves stack is popped and pushed into the RedoMoves stack. Similarly, when the user redoes a move, a value is popped from the RedoMoves stack and re-pushed into the Moves stack.

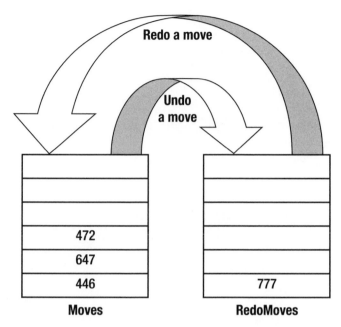

Figure 2-14. *Using stacks for undo and redo options*

Generating the Grid Dynamically

The first thing to do when the application loads is to generate the grid of a Sudoku puzzle. The DrawBoard() subroutine dynamically creates 81 Label controls to represent each cell in the 9×9 grid:

```
'==================================================
' Draw the cells and initialize the grid
'==================================================
Public Sub DrawBoard()
    '---default selected number is 1---
    ToolStripButton1.Checked = True
    SelectedNumber = 1

    '---used to store the location of the cell---
    Dim location As New Point
    '---draws the cells
    For row As Integer = 1 To 9
        For col As Integer = 1 To 9
            location.X = col * (CellWidth + 1) + xOffset
            location.Y = row * (cellHeight + 1) + yOffset
            Dim lbl As New Label
```

```
                    With lbl
                        .Name = col.ToString() & row.ToString()
                        .BorderStyle = BorderStyle.Fixed3D
                        .Location = location
                        .Width = CellWidth
                        .Height = cellHeight
                        .TextAlign = ContentAlignment.MiddleCenter
                        .BackColor = DEFAULT_BACKCOLOR
                        .Font = New Font(.Font, .Font.Style Or _
                            FontStyle.Bold)
                        .Tag = "1"
                        AddHandler lbl.Click, AddressOf Cell_Click
                    End With
                    Me.Controls.Add(lbl)
                Next
            Next
        End Sub
```

Note that as you type the line `AddHandler lbl.Click, AddressOf Cell_Click`, you will get a compiler error, because the method has not been defined yet. For now, let's add an empty `Cell_Click()` method stub so that the compiler does not complain:

```
    Private Sub Cell_Click( _
        ByVal sender As System.Object, _
        ByVal e As System.EventArgs)
          '---content to be populated later---
    End Sub
```

Each Label control is hooked to the `Cell_Click()` event handler, which is fired when the user clicks each Label control (we will declare in it a later section).

The board is first drawn when the form loads, in the `Form1_Load()` event (you can simply double-click an empty portion of `Form1` to create this event handler):

```
    Private Sub Form1_Load( _
        ByVal sender As System.Object, _
        ByVal e As System.EventArgs) Handles MyBase.Load
          '---initialize the status bar---
          ToolStripStatusLabel1.Text = String.Empty
          ToolStripStatusLabel2.Text = String.Empty
          '---draw the board---
          DrawBoard()
    End Sub
```

Figure 2-15 shows what the form looks like when it loads.

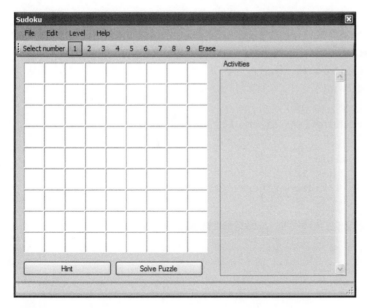

Figure 2-15. *Dynamically generating the Label controls*

One feature is missing, however. In a Sudoku puzzle, nine minigrids are contained within the bigger grid. You need a way to outline the nine minigrids. You do that by actually drawing the lines—four horizontally and four vertically. The Form1_Paint() event is the event that you use to insert the code to draw the eight lines:

```
'=================================================
' Draw the lines outlining the minigrids
'=================================================
Private Sub Form1_Paint( _
    ByVal sender As Object, _
    ByVal e As System.Windows.Forms.PaintEventArgs) _
    Handles Me.Paint

    Dim x1, y1, x2, y2 As Integer
    '---draw the horizontal lines---
    x1 = 1 * (CellWidth + 1) + xOffset - 1
    x2 = 9 * (CellWidth + 1) + xOffset + CellWidth
    For r As Integer = 1 To 10 Step 3
        y1 = r * (cellHeight + 1) + yOffset - 1
        y2 = y1
        e.Graphics.DrawLine(Pens.Black, x1, y1, x2, y2)
    Next
```

```
'---draw the vertical lines---
y1 = 1 * (cellHeight + 1) + yOffset - 1
y2 = 9 * (cellHeight + 1) + yOffset + cellHeight
For c As Integer = 1 To 10 Step 3
    x1 = c * (CellWidth + 1) + xOffset - 1
    x2 = x1
    e.Graphics.DrawLine(Pens.Black, x1, y1, x2, y2)
Next
    End Sub
```

Figure 2-16 shows the effect of drawing these eight lines on the grid.

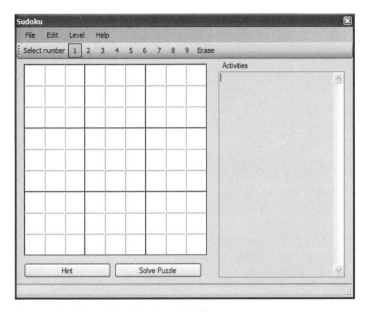

Figure 2-16. *The grid with the eight lines*

Starting a New Game

To start a new game, the user will select File ➤ New. For now, you will simply clear the board and reset a few variables. In Chapter 6, you will be more adventurous and learn how to generate a new Sudoku puzzle of varying levels of difficulty.

When a user starts a new game, be sure to ask if she wants to save the current game. If she does, save the current game before you start a new game. To add an event handler for the New menu item, double-click the New menu item in design view of Visual Studio and the event handler for the New menu item will appear. Code the following:

```
'=======================================================
' Start a new game
'=======================================================
Private Sub NewToolStripMenuItem_Click( _
    ByVal sender As System.Object, _
    ByVal e As System.EventArgs) _
    Handles NewToolStripMenuItem.Click

    If GameStarted Then
        Dim response As MsgBoxResult = _
            MessageBox.Show("Do you want to save current game?", _
                            "Save current game", _
                            MessageBoxButtons.YesNoCancel, _
                            MessageBoxIcon.Question)

        If response = MsgBoxResult.Yes Then
            SaveGameToDisk(False)
        ElseIf response = MsgBoxResult.Cancel Then
            Return
        End If
    End If


    StartNewGame()
End Sub
```

As usual, to prevent the compiler from complaining about the missing
SaveGameToDisk() subroutine, add a stub for this subroutine:

```
Public Sub SaveGameToDisk(ByVal saveAs As Boolean)
    '---content to be populated later---
End Sub
```

The StartNewGame() subroutine simply resets a few variables and updates a Label
control located in the status bar. It also calls the ClearBoard() subroutine, which clears
the values in the grid. The code follows:

```
'=======================================================
' Start a new game
'=======================================================
Public Sub StartNewGame()
    saveFileName = String.Empty
    txtActivities.Text = String.Empty
    seconds = 0
    ClearBoard()
```

```
        GameStarted = True
        Timer1.Enabled = True
        ToolStripStatusLabel1.Text = "New game started"
    End Sub
```

The ClearBoard() subroutine prepares the Sudoku grid for a new game and creates a new instance of the Moves and RedoMoves stack objects:

```
    '=====================================================
    ' Draws the board for the puzzle
    '=====================================================
    Public Sub ClearBoard()
        '---initialize the stacks---
        Moves = New Stack(Of String)
        RedoMoves = New Stack(Of String)

        '---initialize the cells in the board---
        For row As Integer = 1 To 9
            For col As Integer = 1 To 9
                SetCell(col, row, 0, 1)
            Next
        Next
    End Sub
```

Notice that when a new game is started, the Timer control is also enabled so that the clock can start running to keep track of the time elapsed. The Timer1_Click() event is fired every 1 second (which is equivalent to 1000 milliseconds, as set in the Interval property). The elapsed time is displayed in the Label control located in the status bar. To display the elapsed time, add the following event to your code:

■Tip Double-click the Timer control at the bottom of Form1 to reveal this code-behind.

```
    '=====================================================
    ' Increment the time counter
    '=====================================================
    Private Sub Timer1_Tick( _
       ByVal sender As System.Object, _
       ByVal e As System.EventArgs) Handles Timer1.Tick
        ToolStripStatusLabel2.Text = "Elapsed time: " & _
                                     seconds & " second(s)"
        seconds += 1
    End Sub
```

Selecting the Numbers to Insert

Once a new game is started, the user will select a number to insert into the cells. You need to ensure that only one number is selected in the toolbar. The SelectedNumber variable keeps track of which number is currently selected, and if the user clicks the Erase button, the number is saved as a 0. To highlight the number selected by the user in the toolbar, create the ToolStripButton_Click() event:

```
'===================================================
' Event handler for the ToolStripButton controls
'===================================================
Private Sub ToolStripButton_Click( _
    ByVal sender As System.Object, _
    ByVal e As System.EventArgs) _
    Handles _
    ToolStripButton1.Click, _
    ToolStripButton2.Click, _
    ToolStripButton3.Click, _
    ToolStripButton4.Click, _
    ToolStripButton5.Click, _
    ToolStripButton6.Click, _
    ToolStripButton7.Click, _
    ToolStripButton8.Click, _
    ToolStripButton9.Click, _
    ToolStripButton10.Click

    Dim selectedButton As ToolStripButton = _
        CType(sender, ToolStripButton)

    '---uncheck all the Button controls in the ToolStrip---
    '---ToolStrip1.Items.Item(0) is "Select Number"
    '---ToolStrip1.Items.Item(1) is "1"
    '---ToolStrip1.Items.Item(2) is "2", etc
    '---ToolStrip1.Items.Item(10) is "Erase", etc
    For i As Integer = 1 To 10
        CType(ToolStrip1.Items.Item(i), ToolStripButton).Checked = False
    Next

    '---set the selected button to "checked"---
    selectedButton.Checked = True
```

```
        '---set the appropriate number selected---
        If selectedButton.Text = "Erase" Then
            SelectedNumber = 0
        Else
            SelectedNumber = CInt(selectedButton.Text)
        End If
End Sub
```

Notice that the ToolStripButton_Click() event handles multiple events. You can make it handle multiple events by separating with commas the events of each control that you want to handle.

Figure 2-17 shows a number selected in the toolbar.

Figure 2-17. *Selecting a number in the toolbar*

Handling Click Events on the Label Controls

When the user has selected a number in the toolbar and clicks a cell on the grid, the Cell_Click() event is fired. If a cell already contains a fixed value that was part of the original puzzle (as indicated by a Tag property value of 0, which is not erasable), then there is no need to go further. If the Tag property value is 1, you need to determine the cell that was clicked (through converting the Sender object into a Label control and identifying its Name property) and then assign it the appropriate value. You will also push the move into a stack data structure so that the user can undo the move later on. Lastly, you need to also check if the puzzle is solved after the value is placed. All these will be serviced by the Cell_Click() event, which is coded as follows:

```
'===================================================
' Click event for the Label (cell) controls
'===================================================
Private Sub Cell_Click( _
    ByVal sender As System.Object, _
    ByVal e As System.EventArgs)
```

```vb
'---check to see if game has even started or not---
If Not GameStarted Then
    DisplayActivity("Click File->New to start a new" & _
    " game or File->Open to load an existing game", True)
    Return
End If

Dim cellLabel As Label = CType(sender, Label)

'---if cell is not erasable then exit---
If cellLabel.Tag.ToString() = "0" Then
    DisplayActivity("Selected cell is not empty", False)
    Return
End If

'---determine the col and row of the selected cell---
Dim col As Integer = cellLabel.Name.Substring(0, 1)
Dim row As Integer = cellLabel.Name.ToString().Substring(1, 1)

'---If erasing a cell---
If SelectedNumber = 0 Then
    '---if cell is empty then no need to erase---
    If actual(col, row) = 0 Then Return

    '---save the value in the array---
    SetCell(col, row, SelectedNumber, 1)
    DisplayActivity("Number erased at (" & _
    col & "," & row & ")", False)

ElseIf cellLabel.Text = String.Empty Then
    '---else set a value; check if move is valid---
    If Not IsMoveValid(col, row, SelectedNumber) Then
        DisplayActivity("Invalid move at (" & col & _
        "," & row & ")", False)
        Return
    End If
```

```
        '---save the value in the array---
        SetCell(col, row, SelectedNumber, 1)
        DisplayActivity("Number placed at (" & col & _
        "," & row & ")", False)

        '---saves the move into the stack---
        Moves.Push(cellLabel.Name.ToString() _
        & SelectedNumber)

        '---check if the puzzle is solved---
        If IsPuzzleSolved() Then
            Timer1.Enabled = False
            Beep()
            ToolStripStatusLabel1.Text = "*****Puzzle Solved*****"
        End If

    End If
End Sub
```

If the puzzle is solved, a beep will sound and a message will be displayed at the bottom of the screen.

Checking Whether a Move Is Valid

Before a value can be assigned to a cell, you must ensure that the value does not violate the rules of Sudoku. That is, it must be the unique number in its column, row, and minigrid. Figure 2-18 shows the checking that must be performed before a cell can be assigned a value. The square indicates the position to insert the value and the shaded regions indicate the cells to check to ensure that the number is unique in its column, row, and minigrid.

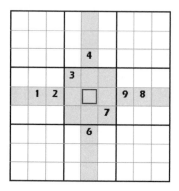

Figure 2-18. *Checking whether a value placed in a location violates the rules of Sudoku*

The IsMoveValid() function checks if a number is valid:

```
'=================================================
' Check if move is valid
'=================================================
Public Function IsMoveValid( _
    ByVal col As Integer, _
    ByVal row As Integer, _
    ByVal value As Integer) As Boolean

    Dim puzzleSolved As Boolean = True

    '---scan through column
    For r As Integer = 1 To 9
        If actual(col, r) = value Then '---duplicate---
            Return False
        End If
    Next

    '---scan through row
    For c As Integer = 1 To 9
        If actual(c, row) = value Then '---duplicate---
            Return False
        End If
    Next

    '---scan through minigrid
    Dim startC, startR As Integer
    startC = col - ((col - 1) Mod 3)
    startR = row - ((row - 1) Mod 3)

    For rr As Integer = 0 To 2
        For cc As Integer = 0 To 2
            If actual(startC + cc, startR + rr) = value Then
                '---duplicate---
                Return False
            End If
        Next
    Next
    Return True
End Function
```

The IsMoveValid() function first scans the nine columns to see if the number to be inserted has already been used. It then proceeds to scan the nine rows, and finally the nine mingrids. At any point in the scan, if a duplicate is detected, the move is deemed to be invalid and the function returns a False.

Checking Whether a Puzzle Is Solved

After a value is assigned to a cell, you need to check if the puzzle is now solved. The IsPuzzleSolved() subroutine checks the entire grid to determine if the puzzle is solved:

```
Public Function IsPuzzleSolved() As Boolean
    '---check row by row---
    Dim pattern As String
    Dim r, c As Integer
    For r = 1 To 9
        pattern = "123456789"
        For c = 1 To 9
            pattern = pattern.Replace(actual(c, r).ToString(),String.Empty)
        Next
        If pattern.Length > 0 Then
            Return False
        End If
    Next

    '---check col by col---
    For c = 1 To 9
        pattern = "123456789"
        For r = 1 To 9
            pattern = pattern.Replace(actual(c, r).ToString(),String.Empty)
        Next
        If pattern.Length > 0 Then
            Return False
        End If
    Next

    '---check by minigrid---
    For c = 1 To 9 Step 3
        pattern = "123456789"
        For r = 1 To 9 Step 3
            For cc As Integer = 0 To 2
                For rr As Integer = 0 To 2
                    pattern = pattern.Replace( _
                        actual(c + cc, r + rr).ToString(), String.Empty)
```

```
                Next
            Next
        Next
        If pattern.Length > 0 Then
            Return False
        End If
    Next
    Return True
End Function
```

The IsPuzzledSolved() function performs checks on the rows, columns, and minigrids. As long as any one of the rows, columns, or minigrids does not have all the numbers from 1 to 9, the subroutine returns a False.

Updating the Value of a Cell

The SetCell() subroutine assigns a value to a cell by specifying its column and row number, the value to set, and whether it is erasable. Because the cells are represented by Label controls generated dynamically, you need to locate a specific cell by using the Find() method in the Controls class. The SetCell() subroutine also sets the cells using the appropriate colors. Code the SetCell() subroutine as follows:

```
'=====================================================
' Set a cell to a given value
'=====================================================
Public Sub SetCell( _
    ByVal col As Integer, ByVal row As Integer, _
    ByVal value As Integer, ByVal erasable As Short)

    '---Locate the particular Label control---
    Dim lbl() As Control = _
    Me.Controls.Find(col.ToString() & row.ToString(), True)
    Dim cellLabel As Label = CType(lbl(0), Label)

    '---save the value in the array---
    actual(col, row) = value
    '---set the appearance for the Label control---
    If value = 0 Then '---erasing the cell---
        cellLabel.Text = String.Empty
        cellLabel.Tag = erasable
        cellLabel.BackColor = DEFAULT_BACKCOLOR
```

```
        Else
            If erasable = 0 Then '---means default puzzle values---
                cellLabel.BackColor = FIXED_BACKCOLOR
                cellLabel.ForeColor = FIXED_FORECOLOR
            Else '---means user-set value---
                cellLabel.BackColor = USER_BACKCOLOR
                cellLabel.ForeColor = USER_FORECOLOR
            End If
            cellLabel.Text = value
            cellLabel.Tag = erasable
        End If
    End Sub
```

Figure 2-19 shows the different color coding used to represent different types of values. The lighter shade indicates values set by the user, while the darker shade represents cells set in the original puzzle.

Figure 2-19. *Setting values in the cells*

The DisplayActivity() subroutine displays a message in the TextBox control. It also accepts an additional parameter indicating if a beep should be sounded. This is useful for displaying error messages to alert the user. Code the DisplayActivity() subroutine as follows:

```
'===================================================
' Displays a message in the Activities text box
'===================================================
Public Sub DisplayActivity( _
    ByVal str As String, _
    ByVal soundBeep As Boolean)
    If soundBeep Then Beep()
    txtActivities.Text &= str & & Environment.NewLine
End Sub
```

Figure 2-20 shows some messages displayed in the Activities TextBox control.

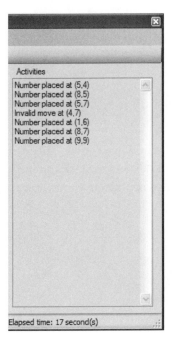

Figure 2-20. *Displaying messages in the TextBox control*

Undoing and Redoing a Move

The user can undo a move by selecting Edit ➤ Undo. To undo a move, you simply need to pop an item from the Moves stack and then push it into the RedoMoves stack. That way, if the user chooses to redo his move, you can retrieve it from the RedoMoves stack as shown in the following event handler for the Undo menu item:

```
'=================================================
' Undo a move
'=================================================
Private Sub UndoToolStripMenuItem_Click( _
    ByVal sender As System.Object, _
    ByVal e As System.EventArgs) _
    Handles UndoToolStripMenuItem.Click

    '---if no previous moves, then exit---
    If Moves.Count = 0 Then Return

    '---remove from the Moves stack and push into
    ' the RedoMoves stack---
    Dim str As String = Moves.Pop()
    RedoMoves.Push(str)
```

```
        '---save the value in the array---
        SetCell(Integer.Parse(str(0)), Integer.Parse(str(1)), 0, 1)
        DisplayActivity("Value removed at (" & _
            Integer.Parse(str(0)) & "," & _
            Integer.Parse(str(1)) & ")", False)
    End Sub
```

To redo a move, a user selects Edit ➤ Redo. This is similar to undoing a move—instead of popping from the Moves stack, you now pop an item from the RedoMoves stack and push it into the Moves stack. The following event handler for the Redo menu item shows how to redo a move:

```
'===================================================
' Redo the move
'===================================================
Private Sub RedoToolStripMenuItem_Click( _
    ByVal sender As System.Object, _
    ByVal e As System.EventArgs) _
    Handles RedoToolStripMenuItem.Click

        '---if RedoMove stack is empty, then exit---
        If RedoMoves.Count = 0 Then Return

        '---remove from the RedoMoves stack and push into the
        ' Moves stack---
        Dim str As String = RedoMoves.Pop()
        Moves.Push(str)

        '---save the value in the array---
        SetCell(Integer.Parse(str(0)), Integer.Parse(str(1)), _
                Integer.Parse(str(2)), 1)
        DisplayActivity("Value reinserted at (" & _
            Integer.Parse(str(0)) & "," & _
            Integer.Parse(str(1)) & ")", False)
    End Sub
```

Saving a Game

Saving a Sudoku puzzle is surprisingly easy. You can save a Sudoku puzzle as a string of digits. For example, the puzzle shown at the beginning of the chapter in Figure 2-1 is saved in a plain text file containing the following string:

```
402000008
000006240
810940007

080697031
006050900
750020080

600213759
003400006
970000400
```

■**Note** I have formatted the string in groups of nine for easy reading. In actual fact, this series of digits is saved in the text file as a one-line string.

The SaveGameToDisk() subroutine first determines if the game has already been saved previously. If it has not been saved before (or if the user selects File ➤ Save As), the Save File dialog box is displayed to allow the user to choose a filename. If the file selected already exists, the SaveGameToDisk() subroutine will delete the file and then create a new one to save the string of digits. Code the SaveGameToDisk() subroutine as follows:

```
'==================================================
' Save the game to disk
'==================================================
Public Sub SaveGameToDisk(ByVal saveAs As Boolean)
    '---if saveFileName is empty, means game has not been saved
    ' before---
    If saveFileName = String.Empty OrElse saveAs Then
        Dim saveFileDialog1 As New SaveFileDialog()
        saveFileDialog1.Filter = _
            "SDO files (*.sdo)|*.sdo|All files (*.*)|*.*"
        saveFileDialog1.FilterIndex = 1
        saveFileDialog1.RestoreDirectory = False
        If saveFileDialog1.ShowDialog() = _
            Windows.Forms.DialogResult.OK Then
            '---store the filename first---
            saveFileName = saveFileDialog1.FileName
```

```
            Else
                Return
            End If
        End If


        '---formulate the string representing the values to store---
        Dim str As New System.Text.StringBuilder()
        For row As Integer = 1 To 9
            For col As Integer = 1 To 9
                str.Append(actual(col, row).ToString())
            Next
        Next


        '---save the values to file---
        Try
            Dim fileExists As Boolean
            fileExists = _
                My.Computer.FileSystem.FileExists(saveFileName)
            If fileExists Then _
                My.Computer.FileSystem.DeleteFile(saveFileName)
            My.Computer.FileSystem.WriteAllText(saveFileName, _
                str.ToString(), True)
            ToolStripStatusLabel1.Text = "Puzzle saved in " & _
                                        saveFileName
        Catch ex As Exception
            MsgBox("Error saving game. Please try again.")
        End Try
    End Sub
```

■**Note** Realize that I used the StringBuilder class for string operation. When manipulating strings in a loop (especially for string concatenation), it is always much more efficient to use a StringBuilder class than to append String objects directly. Also, the My namespace is a new feature in Visual Basic 2005. It is used as a shortcut to the many methods nested deep within the .NET Framework class library.

To save a game, the user can choose File ➤ Save As. The following shows the event handler for the Save As menu item:

```
'=====================================================
' Save as... menu item
'=====================================================
Private Sub SaveAsToolStripMenuItem_Click( _
    ByVal sender As System.Object, _
    ByVal e As System.EventArgs) _
    Handles SaveAsToolStripMenuItem.Click

    If Not GameStarted Then
        DisplayActivity("Game not started yet.", True)
        Return
    End If

    SaveGameToDisk(True)
End Sub
```

If a game has previously been saved, the user can just choose File ➤ Save. The following shows the event handler for the Save menu item:

```
'=====================================================
' Save menu item
'=====================================================
Private Sub SaveToolStripMenuItem_Click( _
    ByVal sender As System.Object, _
    ByVal e As System.EventArgs) _
    Handles SaveToolStripMenuItem.Click
    If Not GameStarted Then
        DisplayActivity("Game not started yet.", True)
        Return
    End If
    SaveGameToDisk(False)
End Sub
```

Opening a Saved Game

To open a previously saved game from disk, you first ask the user if she wants to save the current game. You then invoke the StartNewGame() subroutine and prompt the user to specify the filename of the saved game. You then initialize the individual cells of the grid based on the content of the file opened. The following shows the event handler for the Open menu item:

```vbnet
'=====================================================
' Open a saved game
'=====================================================
Private Sub OpenToolStripMenuItem_Click( _
    ByVal sender As System.Object, _
    ByVal e As System.EventArgs) _
    Handles OpenToolStripMenuItem.Click

    If GameStarted Then
        Dim response As MsgBoxResult = _
        MessageBox.Show("Do you want to save current game?", _
                        "Save current game", _
                        MessageBoxButtons.YesNoCancel, _
                        MessageBoxIcon.Question)

        If response = MsgBoxResult.Yes Then
            SaveGameToDisk(False)
        ElseIf response = MsgBoxResult.Cancel Then
            Return
        End If
    End If

    '---load the game from disk---
    Dim fileContents As String
    Dim openFileDialog1 As New OpenFileDialog()
    openFileDialog1.Filter = _
        "SDO files (*.sdo)|*.sdo|All files (*.*)|*.*"
    openFileDialog1.FilterIndex = 1
    openFileDialog1.RestoreDirectory = False

    If openFileDialog1.ShowDialog() = _
       Windows.Forms.DialogResult.OK Then
        fileContents = _
            My.Computer.FileSystem.ReadAllText( _
                openFileDialog1.FileName)
        ToolStripStatusLabel1.Text = openFileDialog1.FileName
        saveFileName = openFileDialog1.FileName
    Else
        Return
    End If
```

```
        StartNewGame()

        '---initialize the board---
        Dim counter As Short = 0
        For row As Integer = 1 To 9
            For col As Integer = 1 To 9
                Try
                    If CInt(fileContents(counter).ToString()) <> 0 Then
                        SetCell(col, row, _
                            CInt(fileContents(counter).ToString()), 0)
                    End If
                Catch ex As Exception
                    MsgBox( _
                        "File does not contain a valid Sudoku puzzle")
                    Exit Sub
                End Try
                counter += 1
            Next
        Next
    End Sub
```

Ending the Game

To end the game, the user simply chooses File ➤ Exit. Before exiting the application,
prompt the user to save the game. The following shows the event handler for the Exit
menu item:

```
'==================================================
' Exit the application
'==================================================
Private Sub ExitToolStripMenuItem_Click( _
    ByVal sender As System.Object, _
    ByVal e As System.EventArgs) _
    Handles ExitToolStripMenuItem.Click
    If GameStarted Then
        Dim response As MsgBoxResult = _
        MsgBox("Do you want to save current game?", _
        MsgBoxStyle.YesNoCancel, "Save current game")
```

```
            If response = MsgBoxResult.Yes Then
                SaveGameToDisk(False)
            ElseIf response = MsgBoxResult.Cancel Then
                Return
            End If
        End If
        '---exit the application---
        End
    End Sub
```

Testing the Application

Now that the application is all wired up, it is time to test the application. In Visual Studio 2005, press F5 to debug the application.

Save the following in a text file and save it as C:\Easy.sdo:

005400180146080500070013000451008706080000010603700948000390070004070269019006400

In the Sudoku application, load the Easy.sdo file by choosing File ➤ Open and selecting C:\Easy.sdo. The Sudoku puzzle should now look like Figure 2-21.

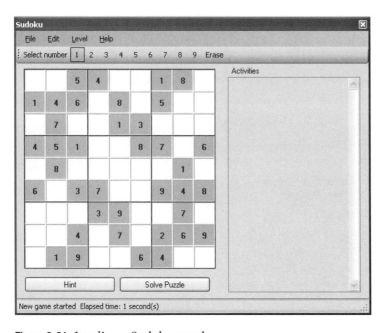

Figure 2-21. *Loading a Sudoku puzzle*

Try solving the puzzle and see how long it takes.

■ **Tip** This is an easy Sudoku puzzle.

Give up? Figure 2-22 shows the solution for the puzzle!

3	9	5	4	6	7	1	8	2
1	4	6	2	8	9	5	3	7
2	7	8	5	1	3	6	9	4
4	5	1	9	3	8	7	2	6
9	8	7	6	4	2	3	1	5
6	2	3	7	5	1	9	4	8
5	6	2	3	9	4	8	7	1
8	3	4	1	7	5	2	6	9
7	1	9	8	2	6	4	5	3

Figure 2-22. *The solution to the Sudoku puzzle*

Summary

In this chapter, you have walked through the various steps to construct a Sudoku puzzle board using a Windows application. This is the foundation chapter that all future chapters will build on. Although the application in this chapter lacks the intelligence required to solve a Sudoku puzzle, it does allow you to play Sudoku on the computer. Moreover, the application that you built in this chapter provides some aid to beginning Sudoku players because it checks for compliance with the rules of Sudoku. Go find a Sudoku puzzle and load it using this application. You will gain a better appreciation of the game after a few rounds.

In the next chapter, you are going to discover the first steps toward programmatically solving a Sudoku puzzle. You will be surprised to learn that a lot of Sudoku puzzles can actually be solved by using the simple logic detailed in Chapter 3.

CHAPTER 3

Basic Sudoku Solving Technique

In the last chapter, you built the user interface for the Sudoku application and added some basic functionality to allow users to play Sudoku puzzles on the computer (although the computer does not have the intelligence to solve Sudoku puzzles yet). Using the Sudoku application, you can load a Sudoku puzzle and use it as a rule enforcer to help you place the numbers in the correct positions. An added benefit of the application is that you can also use it to manually craft Sudoku puzzles, because it allows you to place numbers on an empty grid and then save the game to disk. The saved game can then be shared with your friends.

Beginning in this chapter, we will look at the various techniques that you can use to solve a Sudoku puzzle. For a start, this chapter describes the fundamental technique you can use to solve most of the easy Sudoku puzzles. I first walk you through the technique so that you understand how it works, and then I show you the implementation details.

While the technique covered in this chapter can be used to solve most of the easy Sudoku puzzles, it is not sufficient to solve other, more complex Sudoku puzzles. To help you to accomplish that, I will discuss more advanced techniques in Chapters 4 and 5.

Elimination Technique

Most Sudoku puzzles can be solved by a process of elimination. For example, if eight out of nine cells in a row are filled, then the remaining cell must be the number that has not been used in the row. In the case of Figure 3-1, the value of the remaining cell, (5,1), must be 5, since 1 through 4 and 6 through 9 have already been used in that row.

Note Recall that a cell is identified by its column and row number, so (5,1) refers to the cell in column 5 and row 1.

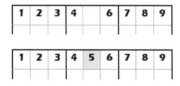

Figure 3-1. *Deriving the number for a cell based on elimination*

When you try to place a number in a cell, examining just its row usually is insufficient, because typically, unlike Figure 3-1, not all the other cells in the row are filled. You have to also scan its column and, if that is not enough, scan within its minigrid. I call this technique *Column, Row, and Minigrid Elimination (CRME)*.

Here is the algorithm for CRME:

```
Scan each cell in the grid from left to right, top to bottom
    For each cell:
        Set possible values for each cell to 123456789
        Scan its column and eliminate the values already present in the
            column
        Scan its row and eliminate the values already present in the row
        Scan its minigrid and eliminate the values already present in
            the minigrid
        If there is only one possible value for the cell, the number for
            the cell is confirmed
Until no more cells can be confirmed
```

Column, Row, and Minigrid Elimination

To see how CRME works, let's start off with the simplest scenario. Figure 3-2 shows a partially filled Sudoku puzzle.

4		3	7	8	5	1	2	6
2								
1								
	5	8						
6	1	4						
7		9						
9								
5								

Figure 3-2. *A partially filled Sudoku puzzle*

Scanning each cell from left to right, top to bottom, the first empty cell you encounter is (2,1). Examining the column that it is in tells you that the possible values left for this cell are 2, 3, 4, 6, 7, 8, and 9 (see Figure 3-3).

■**Note** Yes, I realize that by scanning the row before the column, you can quickly deduce that the value for (2,1) is 9 in this case. However, our program will scan by column first, followed by row, so we will follow the CRME algorithm here for purposes of explanation. When solving the puzzle, it really doesn't matter whether you start scanning by column or by row; the end result is the same.

4		3	7	8	5	1	2	6
2								
1								
	5	8						
6	1	4						
7		9						
9								
5								

Figure 3-3. *Scanning by column*

However, scanning horizontally across the row reduces the number of possible values to one, which is 9, because all the other values have already been used, as shown in Figure 3-4.

4		3	7	8	5	1	2	6
2								
1								
	5	8						
6	1	4						
7		9						
9								
5								

Figure 3-4. *Scanning by row*

Since the only possible value is 9, you can now fill in (2,1) with 9 (see Figure 3-5).

4	9	3	7	8	5	1	2	6
2								
1								
	5	8						
6	1	4						
7		9						
9								
5								

Figure 3-5. *Filling in the value for (2,1)*

Continuing with the scanning, the next empty cell is (2,2). Scanning by its column and row, as shown in Figure 3-6, yields the possible values of 3, 4, 6, 7, and 8.

4	9	3	7	8	5	1	2	6
2								
1								
	5	8						
6	1	4						
7		9						
9								
5								

Figure 3-6. *Scanning by column and row*

By scanning the minigrid next (see Figure 3-7), you see that it already has the values of 1, 2, 3, 4, and 9, so the possible values are now reduced to 6, 7, and 8. Because (2,2) has more than one possible value remaining after we have searched the column, row, and minigrid to eliminate values, the answer is not conclusive. But at least we now know that only the values 6, 7, and 8 are possibilities for (2,2).

■Tip Knowing what are the possible values for a cell is very important in solving a Sudoku puzzle. While cells with more than one possible number cannot be used to solve the puzzle in this chapter, you will learn in the subsequent chapters how to utilize them to solve the puzzle.

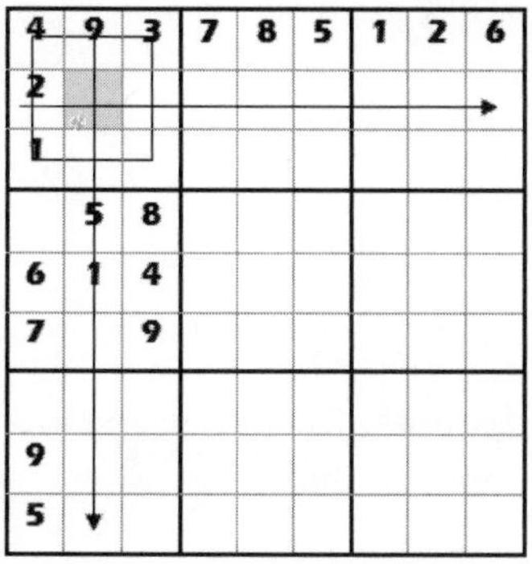

Figure 3-7. *Scanning within the minigrid*

Continuing with the scan, the next interesting cell is (1,4), as shown in Figure 3-8.

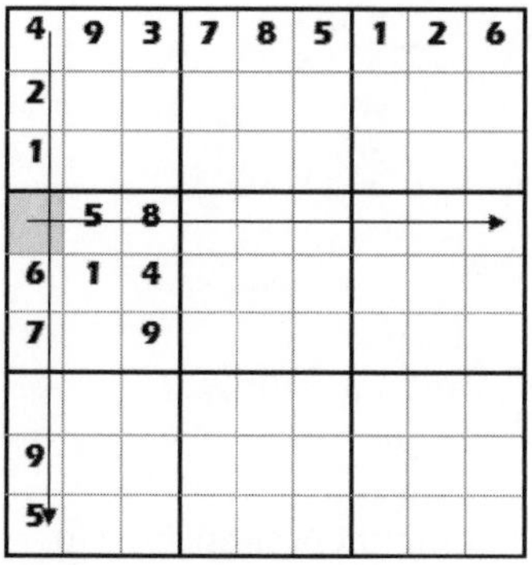

Figure 3-8. *Examining cell (1,4)*

Scanning its column yields 3 and 8 as possible values, but scanning its row confirms that the number is 3. And so you can now fill in (1,4) with 3, as shown in Figure 3-9.

4	9	3	7	8	5	1	2	6
2								
1								
3	5	8						
6	1	4						
7		9						
9								
5								

Figure 3-9. *Filling in (1,4) with the value 3*

Continuing with the scan, the next conclusive cell is (2,6). Scanning by column and row does not yield a specific number, but scanning its minigrid confirms that the missing number is 2 (see Figure 3-10).

4	9	3	7	8	5	1	2	6
2								
1								
3	5	8						
6	1	4						
7	2	9						
9								
5								

Figure 3-10. *Confirming the value for (2,6) by scanning column, row, and minigrid*

This particular cell is worth noting because it illustrates that numbers confirmed in earlier scans (cell (1,4) in this example) can often help in confirming other cells. If you had not previously filled in the number for (1,4), then it would not be possible to confirm the number for (2,6).

Finally, the last cell that you can confirm is (1,7), which you can confirm by simply performing a column scan (see Figure 3-11).

4	9	3	7	8	5	1	2	6
2								
1								
3	5	8						
6	1	4						
7	2	9						
8								
9								
5								

Figure 3-11. *Filling in the value for (1,7)*

Figure 3-12 shows the list of possible values that each cell may contain after running the grid through the CRME algorithm.

4	9	3	7	8	5	1	2	6
2	678	567	13469	13469	13469	345789	345789	345789
1	678	567	23469	23469	23469	345789	345789	345789
3	5	8	12469	124679	124679	24679	14679	12479
6	1	4	23589	23579	23789	235789	35789	235789
7	2	9	134568	13456	13468	34568	134568	13458
8	3467	1267	1234569	12345679	1234679	2345679	1345679	1234579
9	3467	1267	1234568	1234567	1234678	2345678	1345678	1234578
5	3467	1267	1234689	1234679	12346789	2346789	1346789	1234789

Figure 3-12. *Possible values for the rest of the grid*

Usefulness of the CRME Technique

Although the grid in Figure 3-12 shows that a lot of cells are still unconfirmed after running through the algorithm, in reality the situation is much more optimistic, because in a real Sudoku puzzle there are many more initial nonempty cells than illustrated here. After applying the CRME technique to the entire puzzle, you should be able to confirm many more cells.

Also, you should repeat the entire scanning process whenever a cell gets confirmed. To understand why this is important, consider the following. In the previous example, the value for (1,4) was confirmed and later was used to help confirm (2,6). In this case, cells (1,4) and (2,6) were confirmed in one pass, since we are scanning from left to right, top to bottom (see Figure 3-13).

4	9	3	7	8	5	1	2	6
2								
1								
3	5	8						
6	1	4						
7	2	9						
9								
5								

Figure 3-13. *Confirming (1,4) helps confirm (2,6) in single pass*

However, we might not always be that lucky. Consider the puzzle shown in Figure 3-14.

4	9	3	7	8	5	1	2	6
1								
	5	8						
6	1	4						
7		9	1	3		5		
	3							
	4							
	6							

Figure 3-14. *A Sudoku puzzle*

In this case, if you apply the CRME technique to the grid, the first cell to get confirmed is (2,6), which is a 2, as shown in Figure 3-15.

4	9	3	7	8	5	1	2	6
1								
	5	8						
6	1	4						
7	2	9	1	3		5		
	3							
	4							
	6							

Figure 3-15. *First pass only confirms (2,6)*

■Tip This is a good time for you to put what you have learned into practice. Can you see why cell (2,6) is a 2?

But only by putting a 2 into (2,6) can you confirm (1,4). However, as you scan from left to right and top to bottom, by the time you confirm (2,6), you have already passed (1,4). Thus, to derive the value for (1,4), you need to scan the grid one more time, this time confirming (1,4) to be a 3, as shown in Figure 3-16.

4	9	3	7	8	5	1	2	6
1								
3	5	8						
6	1	4						
7	2	9	1	3		5		
	3							
	4							
	6							

Figure 3-16. *Confirming the value for (1,4) in the second pass*

So when do you stop scanning the grid? The answer is obvious—you stop scanning if you can't confirm any cells in a scan (a scan involves 81 cells, from (1,1) to (9,9)). When that happens, you can be sure that this technique has reached its usefulness (if you have not solved the grid by then).

Exception Scenarios

In general, when you apply the CRME technique to a Sudoku puzzle, you can be sure that whenever the possible value for a cell is narrowed down to a single number, the number is confirmed. However, there are two situations that can invalidate this rule:

- The puzzle is invalid
- The user's placement of a number into a cell has caused the puzzle to have no solution

Invalid Puzzle

Consider the seemingly harmless Sudoku puzzle in Figure 3-17.

6		7			1		8	
	8		7				6	9
	3	1		4	5	2		7

Figure 3-17. *A partial Sudoku puzzle that is not solvable*

Applying the CRME technique, the first cell to be confirmed is (1,3), as shown in Figure 3-18.

6		7			1		8	
	8		7				6	9
9	3	1		4	5	2		7

Figure 3-18. *Filling in the value for (1,3)*

But this is where the first sign of trouble shows up. Scanning from cell (8,3), you realize that there is no possible value for it. In its row, the values 1, 2, 3, 4, 5, 7, and 9 are already used, and in its column, 6 and 8 are also taken up. That leaves nothing for (8,3), as illustrated in Figure 3-19.

In this case, the algorithm should sound a warning alarm that there is an error with the puzzle. Unfortunately, at this stage we are not able to detect whether this is a user move error (see next section) or a puzzle that is simply not solvable in the first place.

■ **Tip** To detect whether the puzzle is solvable, you need to solve the puzzle first without any user's moves. Chapter 5 discusses this issue in more detail.

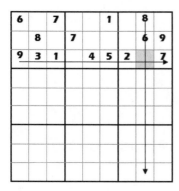

Figure 3-19. *Scanning done in cell (8,3)*

Invalid Move

Whereas you applied the CRME technique to an unsolvable Sudoku puzzle in the previous section, here you begin with a solvable puzzle, shown in Figure 3-20.

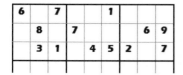

Figure 3-20. *A solvable Sudoku puzzle*

Applying the CRME technique yields the results shown in Figure 3-21.

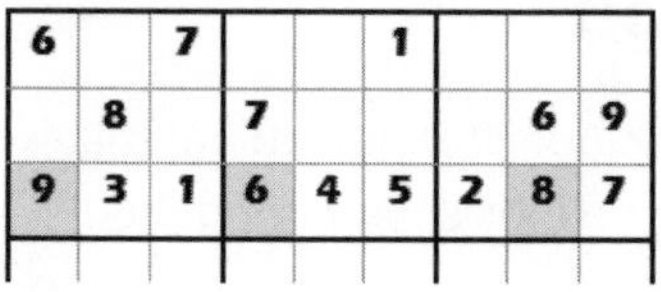

Figure 3-21. *Filling in some of the cells*

However, if the user starts the puzzle with a wrong move, like placing an 8 into (8,1), as shown in Figure 3-22, this causes the puzzle to have no solution.

6		7			1		8	
	8		7				6	9
	3	1	6	4	5	2		7

Figure 3-22. *Getting into a dead end*

Scanning at (8,3) reveals that it has no possible values, as shown in Figure 3-23.

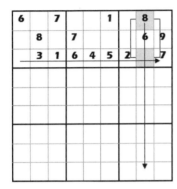

Figure 3-23. *Scanning at (8,3) reveals no possible values*

As in the previous case of an invalid puzzle, the algorithm should sound a warning alarm that there is an error with the puzzle.

Implementing the CRME Technique

Now that you have a good understanding of the CRME technique, it is time to put that into action. This section extends the project created in the previous chapter and then progressively adds the logic to solve the puzzle.

Adding Member Variables

First, add the following member variables to the Form1 class:

```
Private possible(9,9) As String
Private HintMode As Boolean
```

The array possible() keeps track of the possible values for a cell. For example, if the possible values for cell (7,8) are 2, 3, and 5, then possible(7,8) would contain the value 235.

Using the string data type to store the possible values is efficient because it allows values to be removed easily using string manipulation methods such as Replace() in the String class.

The HintMode Boolean variable is used to indicate whether the user is actually requesting a hint or wants the application to solve the entire puzzle. If HintMode is True, as soon as the algorithm confirms a value for a cell, the application stops searching for the number for the next cell and returns control back to the user.

Modifying the SetCell() Subroutine

In the previous chapter, you implemented the SetCell() subroutine to assign a value to a cell. When the value of a cell is erased, you need to reset the possible values of all the other empty cells to an empty string.

Insert the following code in bold into the SetCell() subroutine:

```
'=====================================================
' Set a cell to a given value
'=====================================================
Public Sub SetCell( _
    ByVal col As Integer, ByVal row As Integer, _
    ByVal value As Integer, ByVal erasable As Short)

    '---Locate the particular Label control---
    Dim lbl() As Control = _
    Me.Controls.Find(col.ToString() & row.ToString(), True)
    Dim cellLabel As Label = CType(lbl(0), Label)

    '---save the value in the array
    actual(col, row) = value

    '---if erasing a cell, you need to reset the possible values
    ' for all cells---
    If value = 0 Then
        For r As Integer = 1 To 9
            For c As Integer = 1 To 9
                If actual(c, r) = 0 Then possible(c, r) = _
                    String.Empty
            Next
        Next
    Else
        possible(col, row) = value.ToString()
    End If
```

```
            '---set the appearance for the Label control---
            If value = 0 Then '---erasing the cell---
                cellLabel.Text = String.Empty
                cellLabel.Tag = erasable
                cellLabel.BackColor = DEFAULT_BACKCOLOR
            Else
                If erasable = 0 Then '---means default puzzle values---
                    cellLabel.BackColor = FIXED_BACKCOLOR
                    cellLabel.ForeColor = FIXED_FORECOLOR
                Else '---means user-set value---
                    cellLabel.BackColor = USER_BACKCOLOR
                    cellLabel.ForeColor = USER_FORECOLOR
                End If
                cellLabel.Text = value
                cellLabel.Tag = erasable
            End If
        End Sub
```

The preceding code segment is needed because when a cell is erased, all the possible values for the other cells are no longer valid, and hence you need to recompute them.

Adding a ToolTip Control

To aid the user in solving the puzzle, we will use a ToolTip control to display the possible values for a cell when the user places the cursor over a cell, like that shown in Figure 3-24.

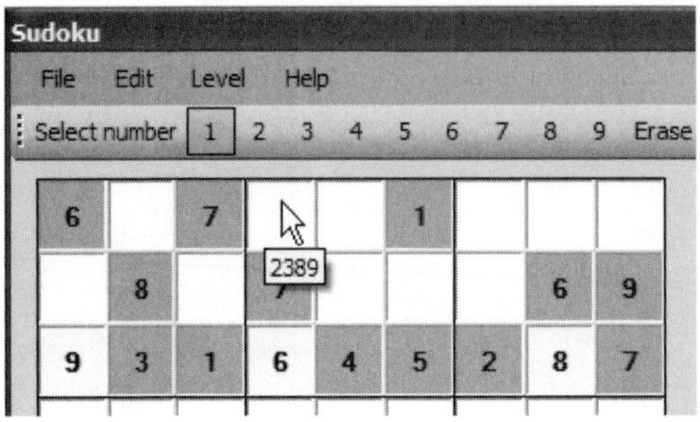

Figure 3-24. *Displaying the possible values for a cell using ToolTip text*

To add a ToolTip control to the application, double-click the ToolTip control (located in the Toolbox under the Common Controls tab) to add it to the project.

Switch to the code behind and add the SetToolTip() subroutine:

```
'====================================================
' Set the ToolTip for a Label control
'====================================================
Public Sub SetToolTip( _
        ByVal col As Integer, ByVal row As Integer, _
        ByVal possiblevalues As String)

    '---Locate the particular Label control---
    Dim lbl() As Control = _
        Me.Controls.Find(col.ToString() & row.ToString(), True)
    ToolTip1.SetToolTip(CType(lbl(0), Label), possiblevalues)
End Sub
```

This subroutine associates ToolTip text (containing the possible values) with the Label control representing the specified cell.

In the StartNewGame() subroutine (created in the previous chapter), add the additional line in bold so that when the user starts a new game, all the current ToolTip associations are removed:

```
Public Sub StartNewGame()
    saveFileName = String.Empty
    txtActivities.Text = String.Empty
    seconds = 0
    ClearBoard()
    GameStarted = True
    Timer1.Enabled = True
    ToolStripStatusLabel1.Text = "New game started"

    ToolTip1.RemoveAll()

End Sub
```

Calculating the Possible Values for a Cell

To calculate the possible values for a cell, you first scan its column, followed by its row, and then the minigrid it is in. If, after scanning, the possible value is an empty string, then the application must raise an exception indicating that an error has occurred. All of these steps are accomplished by the CalculatePossibleValues() function, which returns a string containing a list of possible values for a specified cell:

```vb
'=====================================================
' Calculates the possible values for a cell
'=====================================================
Public Function CalculatePossibleValues( _
                ByVal col As Integer, _
                ByVal row As Integer) _
                As String
    '---get the current possible values for the cell

    Dim str As String
    If possible(col, row) = String.Empty Then
        str = "123456789"
    Else
        str = possible(col, row)
    End If

    '---Step (1) check by column
    Dim r, c As Integer
    For r = 1 To 9
        If actual(col, r) <> 0 Then
            '---that means there is an actual value in it---
            str = str.Replace(actual(col, r).ToString(), String.Empty)
        End If
    Next

    '---Step (2) check by row
    For c = 1 To 9
        If actual(c, row) <> 0 Then
            '---that means there is an actual value in it---
            str = str.Replace(actual(c, row).ToString(), String.Empty)
        End If
    Next

    '---Step (3) check within the minigrid---
    Dim startC, startR As Integer
    startC = col - ((col - 1) Mod 3)
    startR = row - ((row - 1) Mod 3)
    For rr As Integer = startR To startR + 2
        For cc As Integer = startC To startC + 2
```

```
                If actual(cc, rr) <> 0 Then
                    '---that means there is a actual value in it---
                    str = str.Replace(actual(cc, rr).ToString(), String.Empty)
                End If
            Next
        Next

        '---if possible value is an empty string then error because of
        ' invalid move---
        If str = String.Empty Then
            Throw New Exception("Invalid Move")
        End If
        Return str
    End Function
```

Scanning the Grid

The CheckColumnsAndRows() function scans the individual cells in the grid from left to right, top to bottom. It calls the CalculatePossibleValues() function defined in the previous section and then assigns it to the ToolTip control of each Label control. If the possible value returned is a single number, then the number for that cell is confirmed and the cell in the grid is updated with the confirmed number. The Activities TextBox control is also updated with information on the cell that is updated.

If the user is requesting a hint (as indicated by the HintMode variable, which is set in the event handler for the Hint button; see the next section), the subroutine exits after the first successfully confirmed cell. The control is then transferred back to the user.

The implementation of the CheckColumnsAndRows() function is as follows:

```
'=====================================================
' Calculates the possible values for all the cells
'=====================================================
Public Function CheckColumnsAndRows() As Boolean
    Dim changes As Boolean = False
    '---check all cells
    For row As Integer = 1 To 9
        For col As Integer = 1 To 9
            If actual(col, row) = 0 Then
                Try
                    possible(col, row) = CalculatePossibleValues(col, row)
```

```
                    Catch ex As Exception
                        DisplayActivity("Invalid placement, please undo move", _
                            False)
                        Throw New Exception("Invalid Move")
                    End Try

                    '---display the possible values in the ToolTip
                    SetToolTip(col, row, possible(col, row))

                    If possible(col, row).Length = 1 Then
                        '---that means a number is confirmed---
                        SetCell(col, row, CInt(possible(col, row)), 1)

                        '----Number is confirmed
                        actual(col, row) = CInt(possible(col, row))
                        DisplayActivity("Col/Row and Minigrid Elimination",_
                            False)
                        DisplayActivity("=========================", False)
                        DisplayActivity("Inserted value " & actual(col, row) & _
                                    " in " & "(" & col & "," & row & ")",_
                            False)
                        '---get the UI of the application to refresh
                        ' with the newly confirmed number---
                        Application.DoEvents()

                        '---saves the move into the stack
                        Moves.Push(col & row & possible(col, row))

                        '---if user only asks for a hint, stop at this point---
                        changes = True
                        If HintMode Then Return True
                    End If
                End If
            Next
        Next
        Return changes
    End Function
```

The CheckColumnsAndRows() function returns True if there is at least one cell confirmed in a single pass, and returns False if no cells get confirmed.

Wiring the Controls

Now that we have most of the logic worked out, it is time to wire up all the controls. Recall that we have the controls shown in Figure 3-25.

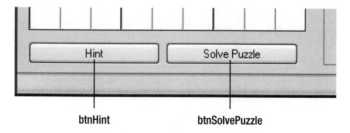

Figure 3-25. *The two Button controls in Form1*

Double-click the Hint button and code the following:

```
'====================================================
' Hint button
'====================================================
Private Sub btnHint_Click( _
    ByVal sender As System.Object, _
    ByVal e As System.EventArgs) _
    Handles btnHint.Click

    '---show hints one cell at a time
    HintMode = True
    Try
        SolvePuzzle()
    Catch ex As Exception
        MessageBox.Show("Please undo your move", "Invalid Move", _
            MessageBoxButtons.OK, MessageBoxIcon.Error)
    End Try
End Sub
```

Likewise, double-click the Solve Puzzle button and code the following:

```
'====================================================
' Solve Puzzle button
'====================================================
Private Sub btnSolvePuzzle_Click( _
    ByVal sender As System.Object, _
    ByVal e As System.EventArgs) _
    Handles btnSolvePuzzle.Click
```

```
        '---solve the puzzle
        HintMode = False
        Try
            SolvePuzzle()
        Catch ex As Exception
            MessageBox.Show("Please undo your move", "Invalid Move",
                MessageBoxButtons.OK, MessageBoxIcon.Error)
        End Try
    End Sub
```

Note that both subroutines call the SolvePuzzle() subroutine, which is defined as follows:

```
'=====================================================
' Steps to solve the puzzle
'=====================================================
Public Function SolvePuzzle() As Boolean
    Dim changes As Boolean
    Dim ExitLoop As Boolean = False
    Try
        Do
            '---Perform Col/Row and Minigrid Elimination
            changes = CheckColumnsAndRows()
            If (HintMode AndAlso changes) OrElse IsPuzzleSolved() Then
                ExitLoop = True
                Exit Do
            End If
        Loop Until Not changes
    Catch ex As Exception
        Throw New Exception("Invalid Move")
    End Try

    If IsPuzzleSolved() Then
        Timer1.Enabled = False
        Beep()
        ToolStripStatusLabel1.Text = "*****Puzzle Solved*****"
        MsgBox("Puzzle solved")
        Return True
    Else
        Return False
    End If
End Function
```

This is the routine that we will modify in subsequent chapters when we add more logic to solve the Sudoku puzzle.

Testing It Out

Testing our algorithm on some real puzzles is the best way to find out how useful it is. Using the puzzle originally shown in Chapter 1 (refer to Figure 1-7), Figure 3-26 shows how the puzzle looks when loaded into our application.

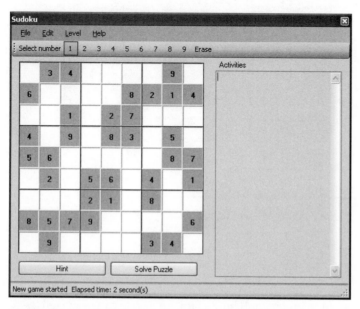

Figure 3-26. *Loading the puzzle shown originally in Figure 1-7*

Of course, if you want to try solving it manually, you can do so using the program. But occasionally, you might want to use the Hint button to get the program to fill in a cell for you. If you are eager to see if our algorithm is powerful enough to solve the puzzle, click the Solve Puzzle button. Presto! The puzzle is solved, as shown in Figure 3-27.

You will be amazed to discover that a lot of Sudoku puzzles can be solved using this CRME technique. If you are in doubt, try using the application built in this chapter and solve some of the puzzles you find in your newspaper.

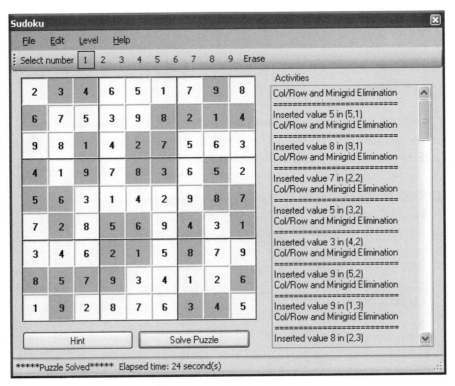

Figure 3-27. *The puzzle solved using the CRME technique*

Summary

In this chapter, you have started to understand how a Sudoku puzzle can be solved by using the elimination technique, which I have named Column, Row, and Minigrid Elimination (CRME).

Of course, the CRME technique has its limitations, and would grind to a stop when applied to more complex Sudoku puzzles. In the next chapter, I am going to show you how you can actually use the information produced by the CRME technique (that is, the possible values for each empty cell) to further solve a Sudoku puzzle.

CHAPTER 4

■■□

Intermediate Techniques

In the previous chapter, you saw how to use the CRME technique to solve some simple Sudoku puzzles. However, there are more-challenging Sudoku puzzles that require much more analysis and new techniques to solve, and that's where the limitations of the CRME technique become apparent. In this chapter, we continue our discovery of new techniques so that we can tackle the more-challenging Sudoku puzzles. Beginning with this chapter and continuing through to the end of the book, we will be looking for some not-so-obvious patterns in Sudoku puzzles and analyzing how we can exploit those patterns to take us one step closer to solving tough Sudoku puzzles.

Lone Rangers

Lone ranger is a term that I use to refer to a number that is one of multiple possible values for a cell but appears *only once* in a row, column, or minigrid. To see what this means in practice, consider the row shown in Figure 4-1. In this row, six cells have already been filled in, leaving three unsolved cells (shown as shaded cells) with their possible values written in them (derived after applying the CRME technique). Notice that the second cell is the only cell that contains the possible value 8. Since no other cells in this row can possibly contain the value 8, this cell can now be confirmed with the value 8. In this case, the 8 is known as a *lone ranger*.

1	348	5	9	6	7	2	34	34

Figure 4-1. *Identifying a lone ranger in a row*

Lone rangers are extremely useful in helping to confirm the number for a cell and are often useful in more complex Sudoku puzzles. Lone rangers can appear in a row, column, or minigrid. Let's see how you can use lone rangers to solve your Sudoku puzzles.

Lone Rangers in a Minigrid

Consider the grid shown in Figure 4-2. We first saw this grid in Chapter 3.

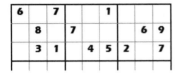

Figure 4-2. *A partial Sudoku puzzle*

Using the CRME technique, we can confirm the values of only three cells, as shown in Figure 4-3.

6		7		1				
	8		7				6	9
9	3	1	6	4	5	2	8	7

Figure 4-3. *Confirming the values of three cells*

We definitely can do better. As a start, let's examine the possible values for all other cells. Figure 4-4 shows the possible values after partially applying the CRME technique.

6	245	7	2389	2389	1	345	345	345
245	8	245	7	23	23	1345	6	9
9	3	1	6	4	5	2	8	7

Figure 4-4. *Possible values for the cells after applying the CRME technique*

One interesting observation is found by looking at the third minigrid, shown in Figure 4-5.

	7	8	9
1	345	345	345
2	1345	6	9
3	2	8	7

Figure 4-5. *Examining the third minigrid*

If you observe cell (7,2), one of the possible values is 1, along with the other numbers like 3, 4, and 5. However, the number 1 appears as a possible value only for (7,2) and not for the other cells within the minigrid. Logically, we can now conclude that *as long as a number appears only once (as a possible value) within the minigrid, that number can be confirmed as the number for the cell.* This is logical, because cells (7,1), (8,1), and (9,1) cannot contain the value 1, and hence only (7,2) can contain 1. Following this argument, we can now put a 1 in (7,2), as shown in Figure 4-6.

6		7			1			
	8		7			1	6	9
9	3	1	6	4	5	2	8	7

Figure 4-6. *Confirming the value for (7,2)*

Lone Rangers in a Row

Lone rangers do not just occur within minigrids; sometimes they occur within rows. Consider the puzzle shown in Figure 4-7.

5	8	3		2			9	
			5	9	3	2		
4	9	2						
		5	7			1		
	6	7				5	3	
		8		5	9			
					5		1	2
		9	2		6			
2	5			8			6	7

Figure 4-7. *Searching a Sudoku puzzle for lone rangers in rows*

Applying the CRME technique yields the list of possible values shown in Figure 4-8.

5	8	3	146	2	147	467	9	146
167	17	16	5	9	3	2	478	1468
4	9	2	168	167	178	3678	578	13568
39	234	5	7	346	248	1	248	4689
19	6	7	148	14	1248	5	3	489
13	1234	8	1346	5	9	467	247	46
3678	347	46	349	347	5	3489	1	2
1378	1347	9	2	1347	6	348	458	3458
2	5	14	1349	8	14	349	6	7

Figure 4-8. *Scanning for lone rangers in rows from the possible values of the unsolved cells*

Scanning for lone rangers in the minigrids does not get you anywhere, but if you look at row 5 (see Figure 4-9), you will see that there is a lone ranger in cell (6,5).

4	9	2	168	167	178	3678	378	13568
39	234	5	7	346	248	1	248	4689
19	6	7	148	14	1248	5	3	489
13	1234	8	1346	5	9	467	247	46
3678	347	46	349	347	5	3489	1	2

Figure 4-9. *Lone ranger detected in row 5*

And that effectively confirms (6,5) with the value 2.

Lone Rangers in a Column

Similar to lone rangers in rows, lone rangers also exist in columns. Consider the example in Figure 4-10.

1	5	8	6					2
	7	2		1		8		6
6			8	2				
	8							
		1		9		2		
	2					3		
8				3	1		2	4
4	1	3		5			7	
2					4		1	

Figure 4-10. *Searching a Sudoku puzzle for lone rangers in columns*

Applying the CRME technique yields the list of possible values shown in Figure 4-11.

1	5	8	6	47	379	3479	49	2
39	7	2	3459	1	359	8	459	6
6	349	49	8	2	3579	134579	459	13579
3579	8	45679	123457	467	23567	145679	4569	1579
357	346	1	3457	9	35678	2	4568	578
579	2	45679	1457	4678	5678	145679	3	15789
8	69	5679	79	3	1	569	2	4
4	1	3	29	5	2689	69	7	89
2	69	5679	79	678	4	3569	1	3589

Figure 4-11. *Scanning for lone rangers in columns from the possible values of the unsolved cells*

If you look at column 8, you will notice that cell (8,5) contains a lone ranger, 8 (see Figure 4-12). And that confirms (8,5) to be 8.

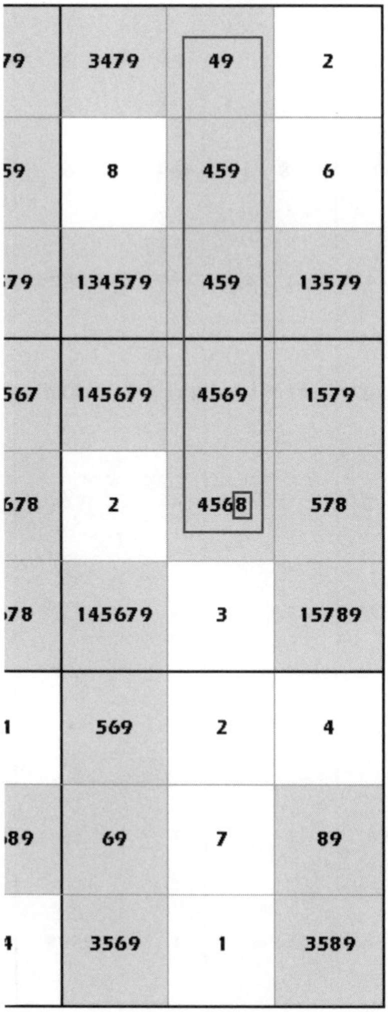

79	3479	49	2
59	8	459	6
79	134579	459	13579
567	145679	4569	1579
678	2	456⊡8	578
78	145679	3	15789
1	569	2	4
89	69	7	89
4	3569	1	3589

Figure 4-12. *Finding a lone ranger in the column*

Once (8,5) is confirmed, you can now apply the CRME technique again, as shown in Figure 4-13. This removes the number 8 from the list of possible values at cells (6,5), (9,5), and (9,6).

1	5	8	6	47	379	3479	49	2
39	7	2	3459	1	359	8	459	6
6	349	49	8	2	3579	134579	459	13579
3579	8	45679	123457	467	23567	145679	4569	1579
357	346	1	3457	9	35678	2	8	578
579	2	45679	1457	4678	5678	145679	3	15789
8	69	5679	79	3	1	569	2	4
4	1	3	29	5	2689	69	7	89
2	69	5679	79	678	4	3569	1	3589

Figure 4-13. *Confirming a cell affects other cells*

And now you will discover yet another lone ranger in the same column, as pointed out in Figure 4-14. And that effectively confirms (8,4) as a 6.

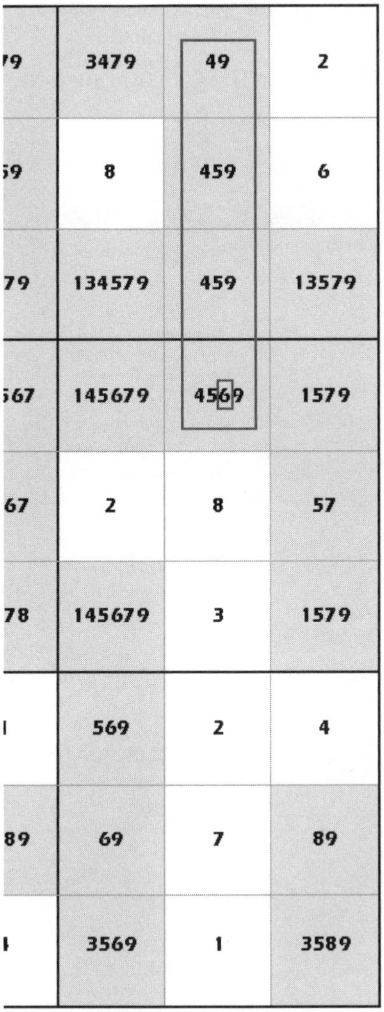

'9	3479	49	2
;9	8	459	6
79	134579	459	13579
;67	145679	45|6|9	1579
67	2	8	57
78	145679	3	1579
I	569	2	4
89	69	7	89
I	3569	1	3589

Figure 4-14. *Confirming yet another cell*

Implementing the Technique

It is now time to implement what we have discussed in code! As usual, we will extend the project used in the previous chapter and progressively apply more puzzle-solving logic to it.

Looking for Lone Rangers in Minigrids

First, we will create the LookForLoneRangersinMinigrids() function. Its mission is to look into each of the nine minigrids and scan for lone rangers (from 1 to 9). If a lone ranger is found, the number is confirmed and the necessary action is taken to insert it into the cell.

The function returns True if a lone ranger is found in one of the minigrids; otherwise, it returns False.

Figure 4-15 shows the steps taken by the LookForLoneRangersinMinigrids() function.

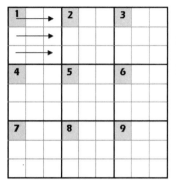

1. Scanning starts from the top left cell of each minigrid (shown labeled from 1 to 9).

2. Each minigrid is scanned from left to right, top to bottom, looking for lone rangers.

3. The entire process is repeated for each of the nine numbers from 1 to 9

Figure 4-15. *Looking for lone rangers in minigrids*

Code the LookForLoneRangersinMinigrids() function as follows:

```
'=====================================================
' Look for Lone Rangers in Minigrids
'=====================================================
Public Function LookForLoneRangersinMinigrids() As Boolean
    Dim changes As Boolean = False
    Dim NextMiniGrid As Boolean
    Dim occurrence As Integer
    Dim cPos, rPos As Integer

    '---check for each number from 1 to 9---
    For n As Integer = 1 To 9

        '---check the 9 minigrids---
        For r As Integer = 1 To 9 Step 3
            For c As Integer = 1 To 9 Step 3

                NextMiniGrid = False
                '---check within the minigrid---
                occurrence = 0
                For rr As Integer = 0 To 2
                    For cc As Integer = 0 To 2
                        If actual(c + cc, r + rr) = 0 AndAlso _
                        possible(c + cc, r + rr).Contains(n.ToString())_
                        Then
```

```
                        occurrence += 1
                        cPos = c + cc
                        rPos = r + rr
                        If occurrence > 1 Then
                            NextMiniGrid = True
                            Exit For
                        End If
                    End If
                Next
                If NextMiniGrid Then Exit For
            Next
            If (Not NextMiniGrid) AndAlso occurrence = 1 Then
                '---that means number is confirmed---
                SetCell(cPos, rPos, n, 1)
                SetToolTip(cPos, rPos, n.ToString())
                '---saves the move into the stack
                Moves.Push(cPos & rPos & n.ToString())
                DisplayActivity("Look for Lone Rangers in Minigrids",_
                    False)
                DisplayActivity("===========================", False)
                DisplayActivity("Inserted value " & n.ToString() & _
                                " in " & "(" & cPos & "," & rPos & ")",_
                    False)
                Application.DoEvents()
                changes = True
                '---if user clicks the Hint button, exit the function---
                If HintMode Then Return True
            End If
        Next
    Next
    Next
    Return changes
End Function
```

■**Note** AndAlso is a short-circuit operator that is new in Visual Basic 2005. When using this operator, if the first condition evaluates to False, the second condition will not be evaluated.

Looking for Lone Rangers in Rows

The next function we will write is the LookForLoneRangersinRows() function. This function scans for lone rangers in each of the nine rows. It starts from the first row and iteratively looks for lone rangers that may be present in the row, until the last row. This function is less complex than the previous function, because the previous function has to scan within a minigrid and hence involves additional looping constructs.

Figure 4-16 shows the steps taken by the LookForLoneRangersinRows() function.

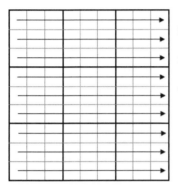

1. Scanning starts from the top row.
2. Each row is scanned from left to right, looking for lone rangers.
3. Step 2 is repeated for each of the nine numbers from 1 to 9
4. Scanning continues on the next row until the last row is completed.

Figure 4-16. *Looking for lone rangers in rows*

Code the LookForLoneRangersinRows() function as follows:

```
'============================================================
'Look for Lone Rangers in Rows
'============================================================
Public Function LookForLoneRangersinRows() As Boolean
    Dim changes As Boolean = False
    Dim occurrence As Integer
    Dim cPos, rPos As Integer

    '---check by row----
    For r As Integer = 1 To 9
        For n As Integer = 1 To 9
            occurrence = 0
            For c As Integer = 1 To 9
```

```
                If actual(c, r) = 0 AndAlso _
                    possible(c, r).Contains(n.ToString()) Then
                    occurrence += 1
                    '---if multiple occurrences, not a lone ranger anymore
                    If occurrence > 1 Then Exit For
                    cPos = c
                    rPos = r
                End If
            Next
            If occurrence = 1 Then
                '--number is confirmed---
                SetCell(cPos, rPos, n, 1)
                SetToolTip(cPos, rPos, n.ToString())
                '---saves the move into the stack---
                Moves.Push(cPos & rPos & n.ToString())
                DisplayActivity("Look for Lone Rangers in Rows", False)
                DisplayActivity("=========================", False)
                DisplayActivity("Inserted value " & n.ToString() & _
                                " in " & "(" & cPos & "," & rPos & ")", _
                                False)
                Application.DoEvents()
                changes = True
                '---if user clicks the Hint button, exit the function---
                If HintMode Then Return True
            End If
        Next
    Next
    Return changes
End Function
```

Looking for Lone Rangers in Columns

The last function we will write is the LookForLoneRangersinColumns() function. This function is almost identical to the LookForLoneRangersinRows() function, except that it scans for lone rangers in each of the nine columns.

Figure 4-17 shows the steps taken by the LookForLoneRangersinColumns() function.

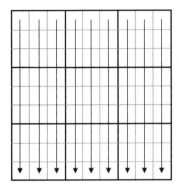

1. Scanning starts from the first column.
2. Each column is scanned from top to bottom, looking for lone rangers.
3. Step 2 is repeated for each of the nine numbers from 1 to 9
4. Scanning continues on the next column until the last column is completed.

Figure 4-17. *Looking for lone rangers in columns*

Code the LookForLoneRangersinColumns() function as follows:

```
'===========================================================
'Look for Lone Rangers in Columns
'===========================================================
Public Function LookForLoneRangersinColumns() As Boolean
    Dim changes As Boolean = False
    Dim occurrence As Integer
    Dim cPos, rPos As Integer

    '----check by column----
    For c As Integer = 1 To 9
        For n As Integer = 1 To 9
            occurrence = 0
            For r As Integer = 1 To 9
                If actual(c, r) = 0 AndAlso _
                    possible(c, r).Contains(n.ToString()) Then
                    occurrence += 1
                    '---if multiple occurrences, not a lone ranger anymore
                    If occurrence > 1 Then Exit For
                    cPos = c
                    rPos = r
                End If
            Next
```

```
            If occurrence = 1 Then
                '--number is confirmed---
                SetCell(cPos, rPos, n, 1)
                SetToolTip(cPos, rPos, n.ToString())
                '---saves the move into the stack
                Moves.Push(cPos & rPos & n.ToString())
                DisplayActivity("Look for Lone Rangers in Columns", False)
                DisplayActivity("============================", False)
                DisplayActivity("Inserted value " & n.ToString() & _
                                " in " & "(" & cPos & "," & rPos & ")",_
                                False)
                Application.DoEvents()
                changes = True
                '---if user clicks the Hint button, exit the function---
                If HintMode Then Return True
            End If
        Next
    Next
    Return changes
End Function
```

■Tip The reason I have three separate functions for scanning lone rangers
(LookForLoneRangersinMinigrids(), LookForLoneRangersinRows(), and
LookForLoneRangersinColumns()) is that a cell that is confirmed during a scan in a
minigrid can cause other cells to be confirmed using the simpler CRME technique. Hence,
after scanning all the minigrids, I apply CRME to the grid and then progressively scan for lone
rangers in columns and rows.

Modifying the SolvePuzzle() Function

To solve a Sudoku puzzle using the lone ranger technique, we first apply CRME to the grid.
If there are no more changes, then we scan for lone rangers in the minigrids. If at least one
cell is confirmed in one of the minigrids, we apply the CRME technique to the entire grid
again. We scan for lone rangers in the rows only when the first two techniques have not
resulted in any changes to the grid. Finally, we scan for lone rangers in columns after
everything else fails to effect any changes on the grid.

Figure 4-18 shows the main flow of the SolvePuzzle() function and how it applies the
techniques discussed to solve the puzzle.

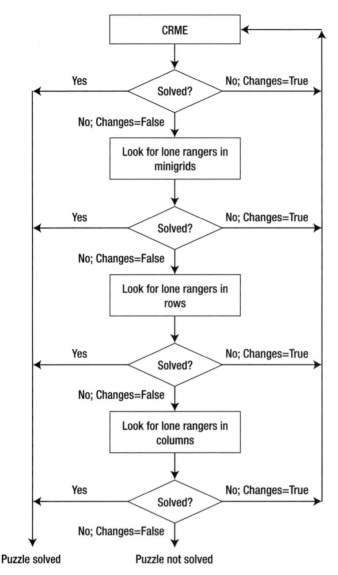

Figure 4-18. *Flowchart showing how various techniques are applied to solve a Sudoku puzzle*

In the SolvePuzzle() function, add the lines in bold to scan for lone rangers:

```
'=================================================
' Steps to solve the puzzle
'=================================================
Public Function SolvePuzzle() As Boolean
    Dim changes As Boolean
    Dim ExitLoop As Boolean = False
```

```
Try
    Do
        Do
            Do
                Do
                    '---Perform Col/Row and Minigrid Elimination----
                    changes = CheckColumnsAndRows()
                    If (HintMode AndAlso changes) OrElse _
                        IsPuzzleSolved() Then
                            ExitLoop = True
                            Exit Do
                    End If
                Loop Until Not changes

                If ExitLoop Then Exit Do
                '---Look for Lone Ranger in Minigrids----
                changes = LookForLoneRangersinMinigrids()
                If (HintMode AndAlso changes) OrElse _
                    IsPuzzleSolved() Then
                        ExitLoop = True
                        Exit Do
                End If
            Loop Until Not changes

            If ExitLoop Then Exit Do
            '---Look for Lone Ranger in Rows----
            changes = LookForLoneRangersinRows()
            If (HintMode AndAlso changes) OrElse IsPuzzleSolved() Then
                    ExitLoop = True
                    Exit Do
            End If
        Loop Until Not changes

        If ExitLoop Then Exit Do
        '---Look for Lone Ranger in Columns----
        changes = LookForLoneRangersinColumns()
        If (HintMode AndAlso changes) OrElse IsPuzzleSolved() Then
                ExitLoop = True
                Exit Do
        End If
    Loop Until Not changes
```

```
        Catch ex As Exception
            Throw New Exception("Invalid Move")
        End Try

        If IsPuzzleSolved() Then
            Timer1.Enabled = False
            Beep()
            ToolStripStatusLabel1.Text = "*****Puzzle Solved*****"
            MsgBox("Puzzle solved")
            Return True
        Else
            Return False
        End If
    End Function
```

Note OrElse is another short-circuit operator that's new in Visual Basic 2005. When using this operator, if the first condition evaluates to True, the second condition will not be evaluated.

Another way of scanning is to scan using CRME first, then scan for lone rangers in minigrids, rows, and columns, and then repeat the entire process. However, my preference is to apply the simpler CRME technique immediately after each scan for lone rangers (minigrids, rows, and columns), because the CRME technique is computationally less expensive than scanning for lone rangers and provides a good chance that the puzzle could be solved directly.

Testing Out the Lone Ranger Technique

With all the relevant pieces of code in place, we can now embark on testing how useful the lone ranger technique is in solving Sudoku puzzles.

Example 1

Consider the puzzle shown in Figure 4-19.

Tip The puzzle is named Chap4-Eg1.sdo and can be downloaded from the book's support site at http://apress.com/book/download.html.

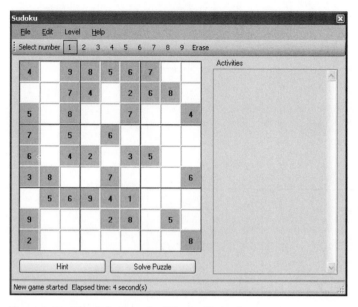

Figure 4-19. *A Sudoku puzzle (Chap4-Eg1.sdo)*

The first step is to apply the CRME technique to see if the puzzle can be solved. Doing so yields the result shown in Figure 4-20.

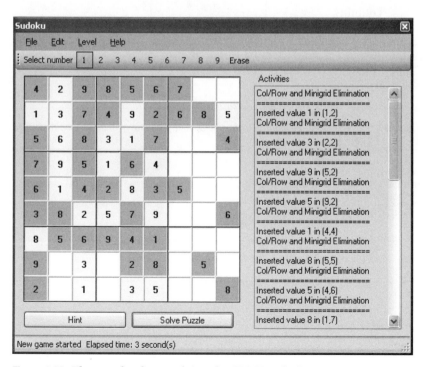

Figure 4-20. *The puzzle after applying the CRME technique*

The possible values for each cell after applying the CRME technique are shown in Figure 4-21.

4	2	9	8	5	6	7	13	13
1	3	7	4	9	2	6	8	5
5	6	8	3	1	7	29	29	4
7	9	5	1	6	4	238	23	23
6	1	4	2	8	3	5	79	79
3	8	2	5	7	9	14	14	6
8	5	6	9	4	1	23	237	237
9	47	3	67	2	8	14	5	17
2	47	1	67	3	5	49	4679	8

Figure 4-21. *Possible values for the cells after applying the CRME technique*

■**Tip** Before you proceed, challenge yourself and see if you can spot any lone rangers in the nine minigrids.

Scanning for lone rangers in the nine minigrids will confirm three additional cells, as shown in Figure 4-22.

■**Note** In this puzzle, there are no lone rangers in the rows or columns.

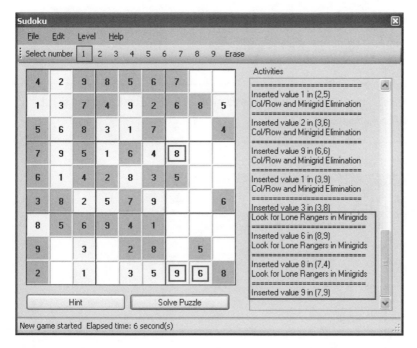

Figure 4-22. *The puzzle after scanning for lone rangers in the minigrids*

Applying the CRME technique to the grid again immediately solves the puzzle (see Figure 4-23).

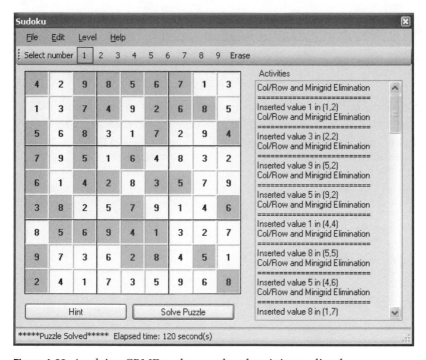

Figure 4-23. *Applying CRME to the puzzle solves it immediately.*

Example 2

Let's consider another example, shown in Figure 4-24.

■**Tip** The puzzle is named `Chap4-Eg2.sdo` and can be downloaded from the book's support site at `http://apress.com/book/download.html`.

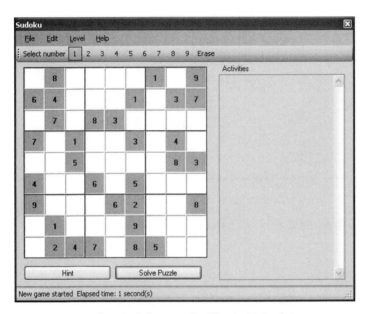

Figure 4-24. *Another Sudoku puzzle (Chap4-Eg2.sdo)*

Applying the CRME technique to this puzzle gives us the state shown in Figure 4-25. Scanning the minigrids, rows, and columns for lone rangers and then applying the CRME techniques iteratively to the grid again yields the result shown in Figure 4-26.

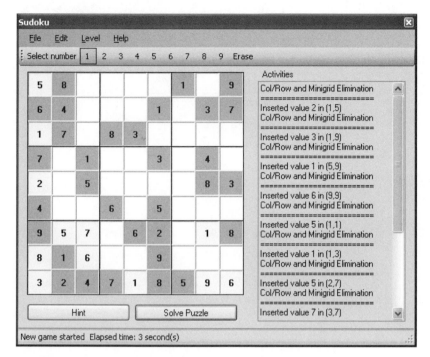

Figure 4-25. *The puzzle after applying the CRME technique*

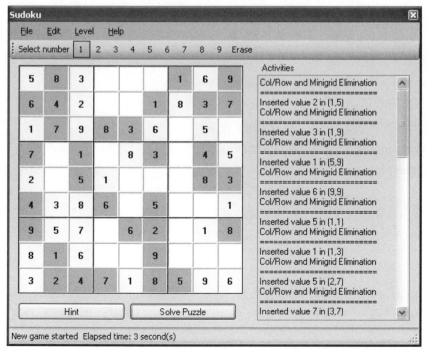

Figure 4-26. *The puzzle after scanning for lone rangers in the minigrids*

Table 4-1 details the steps attempted by the application to solve the puzzle.

Table 4-1. *Steps Taken by the Application to Solve the Puzzle*

Technique Used	Value Inserted
CRME	Value 2 in (1,5)
CRME	Value 3 in (1,9)
CRME	Value 1 in (5,9)
CRME	Value 6 in (9,9)
CRME	Value 5 in (1,1)
CRME	Value 1 in (1,3)
CRME	Value 5 in (2,7)
CRME	Value 7 in (3,7)
CRME	Value 1 in (8,7)
CRME	Value 8 in (1,8)
CRME	Value 6 in (3,8)
CRME	Value 9 in (8,9)
Look for lone rangers in minigrids	Value 1 in (4,5)
Look for lone rangers in minigrids	Value 1 in (9,6)
Look for lone rangers in minigrids	Value 3 in (3,1)
Look for lone rangers in minigrids	Value 5 in (9,4)
Look for lone rangers in minigrids	Value 8 in (7,2)
Look for lone rangers in minigrids	Value 8 in (3,6)
Look for lone rangers in minigrids	Value 3 in (2,6)
Look for lone rangers in minigrids	Value 5 in (8,3)
Look for lone rangers in minigrids	Value 8 in (5,4)
Look for lone rangers in rows	Value 9 in (3,3)
CRME	Value 2 in (3,2)
Look for lone rangers in columns	Value 6 in (8,1)
Look for lone rangers in minigrids	Value 6 in (6,3)

Although applying the CRME and lone ranger techniques did not manage to solve this puzzle, it has significantly weakened the puzzle and reduced the number of empty cells. Figure 4-27 shows the state of the puzzle and the possible values for the nonempty cells. The lone ranger technique sets up the grid nicely and prepares it for solving by using other techniques, which will be discussed in the next chapter.

5	8	3	24	247	47	1	6	9
6	4	2	59	59	1	8	3	7
1	7	9	8	3	6	24	5	24
7	69	1	29	8	3	269	4	5
2	69	5	1	479	47	679	8	3
4	3	8	6	279	5	279	27	1
9	5	7	34	6	2	34	1	8
8	1	6	345	45	9	2347	27	24
3	2	4	7	1	8	5	9	6

Figure 4-27. *State of the puzzle after applying the CRME and lone ranger techniques*

Summary

In this chapter, you learned about the lone ranger technique and how it is useful in helping you to solve or weaken some difficult Sudoku puzzles. Lone rangers are extremely useful and can always help to directly solve a Sudoku puzzle. However, if the techniques covered so far prove ineffective in solving your tough Sudoku puzzles, the next chapter will show you how you can solve the toughest Sudoku puzzles of them all.

CHAPTER 5

■■■

Advanced Techniques

So far, you have learned a couple of techniques that have proven invaluable in solving quite a few Sudoku puzzles. However, some difficult puzzles exist that just refuse to surrender to CRME or lone rangers. In this chapter, you learn three additional techniques that you can use to solve some difficult puzzles: looking for twins, looking for triplets, and, lastly, brute-force elimination, a technique of last resort if everything else fails.

Looking for Twins

To understand the usefulness of looking for twins, consider the partial Sudoku puzzle shown in Figure 5-1, which includes lists of possible values for unresolved cells.

6	245	7	2389	2389	1	345	345	345
245	8	245	7	23	23	1	6	9
9	3	1	6	4	5	2	8	7
1	24	6	5	23	7	8	9	234

Figure 5-1. *A partially solved Sudoku puzzle with the possible values for empty cells*

Observe the two cells (5,2) and (6,2) in Figure 5-2. They both contain possible values of 2 and 3. In this scenario, if (5,2) takes the value 2, then (6,2) must take the value 3. Conversely, if (6,2) takes the value 2, then (5,2) must take 3. All other cells in row 2 besides these two cells cannot contain either 2 or 3. Because the two cells (5,2) and (6,2) have identical lists of possible values and are in the same row, they are known as *twins*.

6	245	7	2389	2389	1	345	345	345
245	8	245	7	23	23	1	6	9
9	3	1	6	4	5	2	8	7
1	24	6	5	23	7	8	9	234

Figure 5-2. *Identifying the twins*

Scanning across the row, you now can eliminate 2 and 3 as possible values for any of the other cells, as shown in Figure 5-3, in which 2 has been deleted as a possible value for cells (1,2) and (3,2).

6	245	7	2389	2389	1	345	345	345
~~2~~45	8	~~2~~45	7	23	23	1	6	9
9	3	1	6	4	5	2	8	7
1	24	6	5	23	7	8	9	234

Figure 5-3. *Eliminating 2 and 3 as possible values for other cells in the same row as the twins*

Similarly, because the twins appear in the same minigrid, all the other cells in this minigrid cannot possibly take the values 2 and 3. Thus, you can eliminate 2 and 3 as possible values for cells (4,1) and (5,1), as shown in Figure 5-4.

6	245	7	23 89	23 89	4	345	345	345
45	8	45	7	23	23	1	6	9
9	3	1	6	4	5	2	8	7
1	24	6	5	23	7	8	9	234

Figure 5-4. *Eliminating 2 and 3 as possible values for other cells in the same minigrid as the twins*

If you noticed, there are now three pairs of twins in the grid, as identified in Figure 5-5. Two pairs are in the first two rows and the third pair is in column 5.

6	245	7	89	89	1	345	345	345
45	8	45	7	23	23	1	6	9
9	3	1	6	4	5	2	8	7
1	24	6	5	23	7	8	9	234

Figure 5-5. *New pairs of twins emerging after the first scanning*

For the twins "23," you can scan the column they are in and remove all occurrences of 2 and 3. For example, if we examine the possible values for column 5, we can see that the values 2 and 3 can be eliminated from many of the cells in this column (shown in Figure 5-6 with the possible values for all the cells in the column).

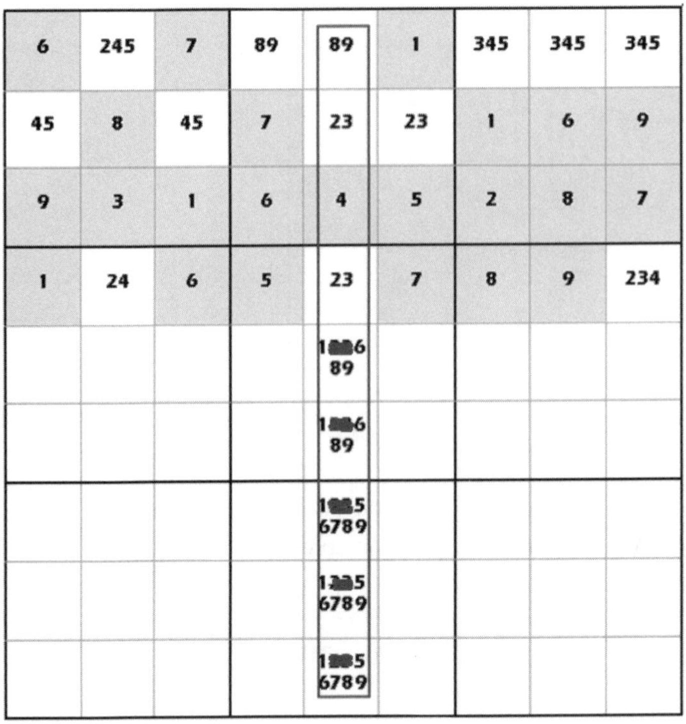

6	245	7	89	89	1	345	345	345
45	8	45	7	23	23	1	6	9
9	3	1	6	4	5	2	8	7
1	24	6	5	23	7	8	9	234
				1■■6 89				
				1■■6 89				
				1■■5 6789				
				1■■5 6789				
				1■■5 6789				

Figure 5-6. *Scanning the column the twins are in*

For the twins "45," scanning by their minigrid allows you to remove the 4 and 5 in cell (2,1), as shown in Figure 5-7. Doing so causes cell (2,1) to be confirmed with 2, which in turn causes (2,4) to be confirmed with 4.

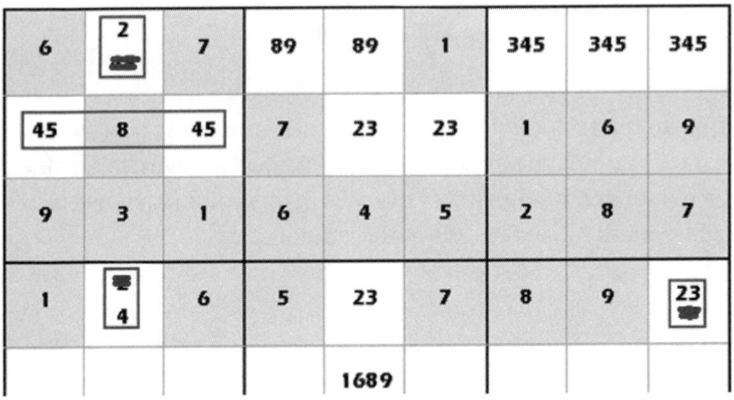

6	2 ■■	7	89	89	1	345	345	345
45	8	45	7	23	23	1	6	9
9	3	1	6	4	5	2	8	7
1	■ 4	6	5	23	7	8	9	23 ■
				1689				

Figure 5-7. *Confirming cell (2,1) and subsequently (2,4)*

For the twins "89," there isn't much you can do to the row and minigrid that they are in. This leaves the grid as shown in Figure 5-8. As you can see, scanning for twins in rows, columns, and minigrids leaves us better off than before the scanning. In our example, two cells get confirmed in the process.

6	2	7	89	89	1	345	345	345
45	8	45	7	23	23	1	6	9
9	3	1	6	4	5	2	8	7
1	4	6	5	23	7	8	9	23
			1689					

Figure 5-8. *The grid after scanning for twins in the rows, columns, and minigrids*

Looking for Triplets

While twins can move you closer to solving a Sudoku puzzle, occasionally you will also come across triplets. Consider the partial Sudoku puzzle shown in Figure 5-9.

1	2467 89	2467 89
246	3	2467 89
246	246	5

Figure 5-9. *A partial Sudoku puzzle*

There are no twins in the minigrid, but you can spot *three* cells with the same possible values. I call these *triplets*. Like twins, triplets are useful in further eliminating possible values for other cells. In the puzzle shown, the numbers 2, 4, and 6 must definitely be placed in one of the three cells containing 2, 4, and 6 as the possible values. Once this reasoning is established, you can cross out the 2, 4, and 6 from the other cells in the mini-grid. The grid now looks like Figure 5-10.

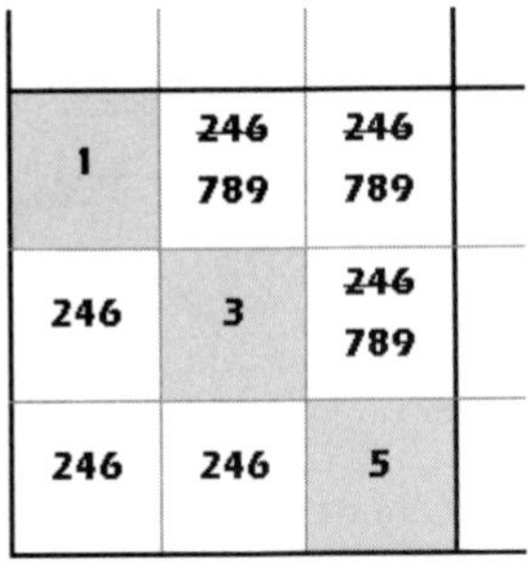

Figure 5-10. *Modifying the minigrid where the triplets are found*

■**Tip** Triplets are made up of three cells.

Although in this example, identifying the triplets did not result in confirming any of the cells, this technique is useful for further reducing the possibilities for other cells, which in turn may be confirmed by some other techniques such as CRME and lone rangers.

■**Note** Like twins, triplets may appear in rows, columns, and minigrids.

Variants of Triplets

In the last section, you saw that triplets are made up of three cells, with each containing the same three possible values. However, this definition is not always strictly adhered to. There are three different scenarios that can be classified as triplets:

- *Scenario 1*: Three cells with the same three possible values (this scenario was discussed in the last section)

- *Scenario 2*: Two cells with three possible values and one cell containing two possible values that are a subset of the three possible values

- *Scenario 3*: One cell with three possible values and two cells containing two possible values that are a subset of the three possible values

It is important to identify the three scenarios, because you have to write code to look out for the various variants of triplets. To understand the three different scenarios, let's consider the following examples.

Scenario 1

The first scenario is the most obvious. As long as three cells have an identical set of three possible values, they are deemed to be triplets, as shown in Figure 5-11. You can then eliminate the triplets as possible values from the rest of the cells.

123	123	123
X	X	X
X	X	X

Figure 5-11. *A set of triplets*

■**Note** In this and the next two scenarios, I have placed the numbers in the first row for ease of explanation. In reality, triplets can occur in rows, columns, and minigrids.

Scenario 2

The second scenario is less obvious: two cells with three possible values and one cell containing two possible values that are a subset of the three possible values. Three examples are shown in Figure 5-12.

123	123	23
X	X	X
X	X	X

123	123	13
X	X	X
X	X	X

123	123	12
X	X	X
X	X	X

Figure 5-12. *Examples of triplets—two cells with three possible values and one cell with two possible values*

■**Tip** The reason why I have shown three examples in Figure 5-12 is that for the cell with two possible values, any combination of the three possible values is valid. In the example, the three possible values in the other two cells are 1, 2, and 3. Hence, for the cell with two possible values, its possible value can be 23, 13, or 12.

To clarify why the examples in Figure 5-12 can be classified as triplets, let's walk through another example. Starting with the first (leftmost) example in Figure 5-12, assume that the third cell now takes the value 2. That causes the first two cells to become twins, with possible values 1 and 3, as shown in Figure 5-13. (The same happens if you now assume that the third cell takes the value 3, which leaves the first two cells with twins, 1 and 2.) Based on the earlier discussion on twins, the first two cells must assume one of the other possible values.

123	123	23		13	13	2
X	X	X		X	X	X
X	X	X		X	X	X

Figure 5-13. *Verifying an example of triplets*

Effectively, this ensures that the three cells must contain one of the three possible values: 1, 2, or 3. All other cells that contain 1, 2, or 3 as possible values must now be eliminated from their list of possible values.

Scenario 3

The third scenario is even less obvious than the second scenario. Figure 5-14 shows two such examples.

123	13	12		123	13	23
X	X	X		X	X	X
X	X	X		X	X	X

Figure 5-14. *Two more instances of triplets—one cell with three possible values and two cells with two possible values*

Using the first (left) example for illustration, suppose the second cell takes the value 1, as shown in Figure 5-15. This causes the third cell to be 2, which in turn causes the first cell to be 3. Hence, the three cells must contain one of the three possible values, 1, 2, or 3.

123	13	12	3	1	2
X	X	X	X	X	X
X	X	X	X	X	X

Figure 5-15. *Trying out the first example*

■ **Tip** Go ahead and assume different values for each of the cells. Each time, you will see that the first three cells must assume either one of the three values 1, 2, or 3.

Brute-Force Elimination

Up to this point, you should be able to solve most Sudoku puzzles using the techniques described in this book. However, sometimes (especially for difficult puzzles) all the techniques seem to be useless. In such cases, you really need to make an educated guess and put a value in a cell and then apply all the techniques covered so far. I call this technique *brute-force elimination.*

Consider the partially solved Sudoku puzzle shown in Figure 5-16. Applying all the other techniques could not solve the puzzle.

		6		7	4	1	2	
		2		8	1	4	6	
1	9	4	2	6	3	8	7	5
6	2	9	3		5	7		
	5	7			6	3	9	
3		1	7	9		6	5	
9	1	3	6	5	7	2		
		5				9	3	6
2	6	8	4	3	9	5	1	7

Figure 5-16. *A partially solved Sudoku puzzle*

Figure 5-17 shows the list of possible values for each of the unsolved cells.

58	38	6	59	7	4	1	2	39
57	37	2	59	8	1	4	6	39
1	9	4	2	6	3	8	7	5
6	2	9	3	14	5	7	48	148
48	5	7	18	124	6	3	9	1248
3	48	1	7	9	28	6	5	248
9	1	3	6	5	7	2	48	48
47	47	5	18	12	28	9	3	6
2	6	8	4	3	9	5	1	7

Figure 5-17. *A partially solved Sudoku puzzle with its lists of possible values*

The most natural way to solve the puzzle would be to do some guesswork. You can select a value for an unsolved cell and apply the earlier techniques to see if that will solve the puzzle. If that doesn't solve the puzzle, select a value for the next unsolved cell and repeat the same process until the puzzle is solved.

Now, the question is: which cell do we start with? Well, quite obviously you should start with the cell with the least number of possible values. Scanning from left to right, top to bottom, you can see that cell (1,1) is the first choice. In (1,1) there are two possible values, 5 and 8. You can choose either 5 or 8, but for simplicity you can always start with the first number. So let's choose 5 for (1,1) and then proceed to solve the puzzle using the techniques we have discussed. Voila! The puzzle is solved, as shown in Figure 5-18.

■**Tip** Always start with the cell with the least number of possible values. That way, you greatly increase the possibility of selecting the correct number that can help to solve the puzzle.

5	8	6	9	7	4	1	2	3
7	3	2	5	8	1	4	6	9
1	9	4	2	6	3	8	7	5
6	2	9	3	4	5	7	8	1
8	5	7	1	2	6	3	9	4
3	4	1	7	9	8	6	5	2
9	1	3	6	5	7	2	4	8
4	7	5	8	1	2	9	3	6
2	6	8	4	3	9	5	1	7

Figure 5-18. *The solved puzzle*

In this example, we are pretty lucky. Simply selecting a cell and assigning a value to it solved the entire puzzle. However, sometimes you will need to select a number, run through the techniques, and then select another cell and run through the same process again. For difficult puzzles, you may need to repeat this several times.

Sometimes, you may just make the wrong decisions and cause the puzzle to be unsolvable. Using the same example, suppose that the first cell we select is not (1,1) but (5,4), with possible values of 1 and 4. Assuming that we selected 1 for (5,4), run the grid through all the various techniques.

Figure 5-19 shows the result of the grid after assigning 1 to cell (5,4) and then using the other techniques to derive other cells.

		6		7	4	1	2	
		2		8	1	4	6	
1	9	4	2	6	3	8	7	5
6	2	9	3	1	5	7		
4	5	7	8		6	3	9	
3		1	7	9	2	6	5	
9	1	3	6	5	7	2		
		5	1	2	8	9	3	6
2	6	8	4	3	9	5	1	7

Figure 5-19. *The state of the grid after assigning 1 to cell (5,4)*

At this stage, an error will occur. If you apply the CRME technique to cell (5,5), you will realize that cell (5,5) has no possible values. Scanning its row and column, all the numbers from 1 to 9 have already been used, as shown in Figure 5-20.

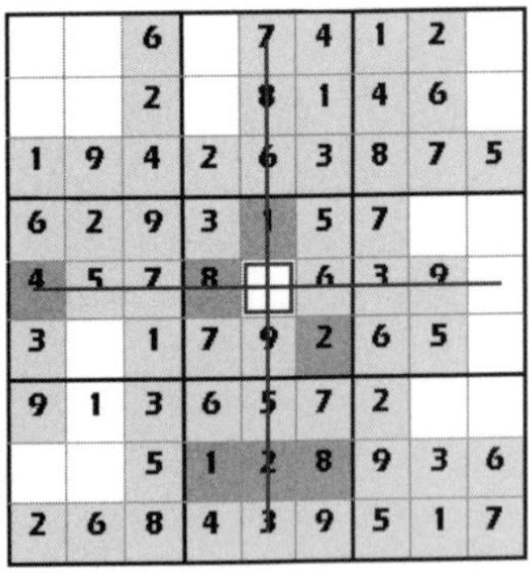

Figure 5-20. *A deadlock situation for cell (5,5)*

In this case, you need to backtrack. You need to backtrack to where you have previously guessed a value. In this case, you need to backtrack to cell (5,4) and, in the process, erase all the cells you have confirmed based on assigning 1 to (5,4). Now, instead of assigning 1 to (5,4), try the next number, 4. This time around, if you apply all the techniques you have learned, you will solve the puzzle.

Based on the description of the brute-force elimination technique, observe the following:

- The brute-force elimination technique can be implemented programmatically using recursion. To allow for moves to backtrack, you need to "remember" the state of the grid before assigning a value to a cell, which enables you to restore the grid to its previous state.

- Selecting the right number to assign to a cell is important. In the example, selecting a 1 for (5,4) causes the puzzle to have no solution, but selecting 4 for (5,4) solves the puzzle. To solve a puzzle, you can always start from the first possible number and work your way toward the solution. To minimize the possibility of backtracks, always select the cell with the least number of possible values when applying the brute-force technique.

- Even though I call this technique brute-force elimination, solving the puzzle using this technique does not imply that we are solving the entire puzzle by guesswork. In fact, for most puzzles, you need to apply the brute-force elimination technique only a few times, and then you can solve the rest of the grid by other logical techniques covered in this book.

Implementing the Techniques

Now that you understand the various advanced techniques described in this chapter, it is time to implement them in code.

Looking for Twins in Minigrids

The first technique that we will implement is the LookForTwinsinMinigrids() function to look for twins in each of the nine minigrids. The function scans through all the cells in the grid and looks for cells with two possible values. Once it finds a cell with two possible values, it searches for the cell's twin in the minigrid that it is in. If there is indeed a pair of twins in the minigrid, the rest of the cells in the minigrid will have their list of possible values modified to remove the values of the twins. After the process, if there are cells left with one possible value, then those cells are confirmed. The function returns a True value if there are any changes to the list of possible values for any of the cells in the grid. It returns a False value if none of the cells' possible values is affected.

Code the LookForTwinsinMinigrids() function as follows:

```
'============================================================
' Look for twins in minigrids
'============================================================
Public Function LookForTwinsinMinigrids() As Boolean
    Dim changes As Boolean = False

    '---look for twins in each cell---
    For r As Integer = 1 To 9
        For c As Integer = 1 To 9

            '---if two possible values, check for twins---
            If actual(c, r) = 0 AndAlso possible(c, r).Length = 2 Then

                '---scan by the minigrid that the current cell is in
                Dim startC, startR As Integer
                startC = c - ((c - 1) Mod 3)
                startR = r - ((r - 1) Mod 3)

                For rr As Integer = startR To startR + 2
                    For cc As Integer = startC To startC + 2

                        '---for cells other than the pair of twins---
                        If (Not ((cc = c) AndAlso (rr = r))) AndAlso _
                            possible(cc, rr) = possible(c, r) Then

                            '---twins found---
                            DisplayActivity("Twins found in minigrid at: (" & _
                                        c & "," & r & ") and (" & _
                                        cc & "," & rr & ")", False)
```

```vbnet
                            '---remove the twins from all the other possible
                            ' values in the minigrid---
                            For rrr As Integer = startR To startR + 2
                                For ccc As Integer = startC To startC + 2

                                    '---only check for empty cells---
                                    If actual(ccc, rrr) = 0 AndAlso _
                                        possible(ccc, rrr) <> possible(c, r) _
                                        Then

                                        '---save a copy of the original
                                        ' possible values (twins)---
                                        Dim original_possible As String = _
                                            possible(ccc, rrr)

                                        '---remove first twin number from
                                        ' possible values---
                                        possible(ccc, rrr) = _
                                            possible(ccc, rrr).Replace( _
                                            possible(c, r)(0), String.Empty)

                                        '---remove second twin number from
                                        ' possible values---
                                        possible(ccc, rrr) = _
                                            possible(ccc, rrr).Replace( _
                                            possible(c, r)(1), String.Empty)

                                        '---set the ToolTip---
                                        SetToolTip( _
                                            ccc, rrr, possible(ccc, rrr))

                                        '---if the possible values are
                                        ' modified, then set the changes
                                        ' variable to True to indicate that
                                        ' the possible values of cells in the
                                        ' minigrid have been modified---
                                        If original_possible <> _
                                            possible(ccc, rrr) Then
                                                changes = True
                                        End If
```

```vbnet
                    '---if possible value reduces to empty
                    ' string, then the user has placed a
                    ' move that results in the puzzle being
                    ' not solvable---
                    If possible(ccc, rrr) = String.Empty _
                      Then
                        Throw New Exception("Invalid Move")
                    End If

                    '---if left with 1 possible value for
                    ' the current cell, cell is
                    ' confirmed---
                    If possible(ccc, rrr).Length = 1 Then
                        SetCell(ccc, rrr, _
                            CInt(possible(ccc, rrr)), 1)
                        SetToolTip( _
                            ccc, rrr, possible(ccc, rrr))
                        '---saves the move into the stack
                        Moves.Push( _
                            ccc & rrr & possible(ccc, rrr))
                        DisplayActivity( _
                            "Look For Twins in Minigrids", _
                            False)
                        DisplayActivity( _
                            "===========================", _
                            False)
                        DisplayActivity( _
                            "Inserted value " & _
                            actual(ccc, rrr) & _
                            " in " & "(" & ccc & "," & _
                            rrr & ")", False)
                        Application.DoEvents()
                        '---if user clicks the Hint button,
                        'exit the function---
                        If HintMode Then Return True
                    End If
                End If
            Next
        Next
    End If
    Next
Next
```

```
            End If
        Next
    Next
    Return changes
End Function
```

If you examine the preceding code, you will realize that the code will scan each individual cell in the grid. If a cell has two possible values, a scan for its twin is made within the
minigrid that it is in. Scanning in the minigrid starts from the top-left corner of the minigrid and continues until the last cell in the minigrid, as shown in Figure 5-21.

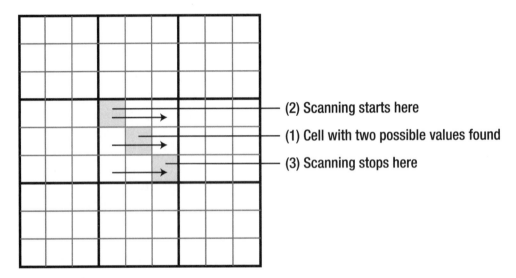

Figure 5-21. *Scanning for twins within a minigrid*

For example, if cell (5,5) has two possible values, then the scanning starts from the first
cell in the minigrid, whose coordinates are derived using the following statements:

```
startC = c - ((c - 1) Mod 3)
startR = r - ((r - 1) Mod 3)
```

Because c = 5 and r = 5, using the preceding formula, you can get startC = 5 –(4Mod3),
which is 4. The same calculation applies to startR, which is also 4. This formula can be
applied to any cells in the grid to derive the coordinates of the starting cell in the minigrid.

Looking for Twins in Rows

The LookForTwinsinRows() function is similar to the LookForTwinsinMinigrids() function except that it scans for twins in the rows. It examines each row and scans its columns from left to right for twins. As soon as it locates a cell with two possible values, it scans starting from the next column until it reaches the last column. If there is indeed a pair of twins in the row, the rest of the cells in the row will have their list of possible values modified to eliminated the values of the twins. After the process, if there are cells left with one possible value, those cells are confirmed.

Code the LookForTwinsinRows() function as follows:

```
'=============================================================
' Look for twins in rows
'=============================================================
Public Function LookForTwinsinRows() As Boolean
    Dim changes As Boolean = False

    '---for each row, check each column in the row---
    For r As Integer = 1 To 9
        For c As Integer = 1 To 9

            '---if two possible values, check for twins---
            If actual(c, r) = 0 AndAlso possible(c, r).Length = 2 Then

                '--scan columns in this row---
                For cc As Integer = c + 1 To 9
                    If (possible(cc, r) = possible(c, r)) Then

                        '--twins found---
                        DisplayActivity("Twins found in row at: (" & _
                            c & "," & r & ") and (" & cc & "," & r & ")", _
                            False)

                        '---remove the twins from all the other possible
                        ' values in the column---
                        For ccc As Integer = 1 To 9
                            If (actual(ccc, r) = 0) AndAlso (ccc <> c) _
                                AndAlso (ccc <> cc) Then
```

```
'---save a copy of the original possible
' values (twins)---
Dim original_possible As String = _
    possible(ccc, r)

'---remove first twin number from possible
' values---
possible(ccc, r) = possible(ccc, r).Replace( _
    possible(c, r)(0), String.Empty)

'---remove second twin number from possible
' values---
possible(ccc, r) = possible(ccc, r).Replace( _
    possible(c, r)(1), String.Empty)

'---set the ToolTip---
SetToolTip(ccc, r, possible(ccc, r))

'---if the possible values are modified, then
' set the changes variable to True to indicate
' that the possible values of cells in the
' minigrid have been modified---
If original_possible <> possible(ccc, r) Then
        changes = True
End If

'---if possible value reduces to empty string,
' then the user has placed a move that results
' in the puzzle being not solvable---
If possible(ccc, r) = String.Empty Then
        Throw New Exception("Invalid Move")
End If

'---if left with 1 possible value for the
' current cell, cell is confirmed---
If possible(ccc, r).Length = 1 Then
        SetCell(ccc, r, CInt(possible(ccc, r)), 1)
        SetToolTip(ccc, r, possible(ccc, r))
```

```
                                   '---saves the move into the stack
                                   Moves.Push(ccc & r & possible(ccc, r))
                                   DisplayActivity("Look For Twins in Rows)", _
                                      False)
                                   DisplayActivity("======================", _
                                      False)
                                   DisplayActivity("Inserted value " & _
                                      actual(ccc, r) & " in " & "(" & _
                                      ccc & "," & r & ")", False)
                                   Application.DoEvents()

                                   '---if user clicks the Hint button, exit
                                   ' the function---
                                   If HintMode Then Return True
                                End If
                             End If
                          Next
                       End If
                 Next
              End If
           Next
        Next
        Return changes
     End Function
```

Figure 5-22 shows the process of scanning for twins in a row.

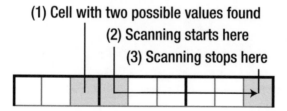

(1) Cell with two possible values found

(2) Scanning starts here

(3) Scanning stops here

Figure 5-22. *Scanning for twins in a row*

The LookForTwinsinRows() function returns True if there are any changes to the list of possible values for any of the cells in the grid. It returns False if none of the cells' possible values is affected.

Looking for Twins in Columns

The LookForTwinsinColumns() function scans for twins in each of the nine columns. It examines each column and scans its rows from top to bottom for twins. As soon as it locates a cell with two possible values, it scans starting from the next row until it reaches the last row. If there is indeed a pair of twins in the column, the rest of the cells in the column will have their list of possible values modified to eliminate the values of the twins. After the process, if there are cells left with one possible value, those cells are confirmed.

Code the LookForTwinsinColumns() function as follows:

```
'=============================================================
' Look for twins in columns
'=============================================================
Public Function LookForTwinsinColumns() As Boolean
    Dim changes As Boolean = False

    '---for each column, check each row in the column---
    For c As Integer = 1 To 9
        For r As Integer = 1 To 9

            '---if two possible values, check for twins---
            If actual(c, r) = 0 AndAlso possible(c, r).Length = 2 Then

                '--scan rows in this column---
                For rr As Integer = r + 1 To 9

                    If (possible(c, rr) = possible(c, r)) Then

                        '--twins found---
                        DisplayActivity("Twins found in column at: (" & _
                            c & "," & r & ") and (" & c & "," & rr & ")", False)

                        '---remove the twins from all the other possible
                        ' values in the row---
                        For rrr As Integer = 1 To 9

                            If (actual(c, rrr) = 0) AndAlso (rrr <> r) _
                                AndAlso (rrr <> rr) Then

                                '---save a copy of the original possible
                                ' values (twins)---
                                Dim original_possible As String = _
                                    possible(c, rrr)
```

```vbnet
'---remove first twin number from possible
' values---
possible(c, rrr) = possible(c, rrr).Replace( _
   possible(c, r)(0), String.Empty)


'---remove second twin number from possible
' values---
possible(c, rrr) = possible(c, rrr).Replace( _
   possible(c, r)(1), String.Empty)


'---set the ToolTip---
SetToolTip(c, rrr, possible(c, rrr))


'---if the possible values are modified, then
' set the changes variable to True to indicate
' that the possible values of cells in the
' minigrid have been modified---
If original_possible <> possible(c, rrr) Then
    changes = True
End If


'---if possible value reduces to empty string,
' then the user has placed a move that results
' in the puzzle being not solvable---
If possible(c, rrr) = String.Empty Then
    Throw New Exception("Invalid Move")
End If


'---if left with 1 possible value for the
' current cell, cell is confirmed---
If possible(c, rrr).Length = 1 Then
    SetCell(c, rrr, CInt(possible(c, rrr)), 1)
    SetToolTip(c, rrr, possible(c, rrr))
    '---saves the move into the stack
    Moves.Push(c & rrr & possible(c, rrr))
    DisplayActivity( _
        "Looking for twins (by column)", False)
    DisplayActivity( _
        "=============================", False)
```

```
                                        DisplayActivity( _
                                            "Inserted value " & actual(c, rrr) & _
                                            " in " & "(" & c & "," & rrr & ")", _
                                            False)
                                        Application.DoEvents()

                                        '---if user clicks the Hint button,
                                        'exit the function---
                                        If HintMode Then Return True
                                    End If
                                End If
                            Next
                        End If
                    Next
                End If
            Next
        Next
        Return changes
    End Function
```

Figure 5-23 shows the process of scanning for twins in a column.

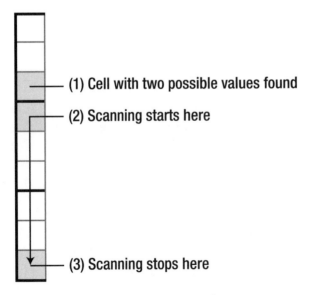

Figure 5-23. *Scanning for twins in a column*

The `LookForTwinsinColumns()` function returns `True` if there are any changes to the list of possible values for any of the cells in the grid. It returns `False` if none of the cells' possible values is affected.

Looking for Triplets in Minigrids

The `LookForTripletsinMinigrids()` function scans through all the cells in the grid and looks for cells with three possible values. Once it finds a cell with three possible values, it searches for two other triplets in the minigrid that the cell is in. If there is indeed a set of triplets in the minigrid, the rest of the cells in the minigrid will have their list of possible values modified to eliminate the values of the triplets. After the process, if there are cells left with one possible value, then those cells are confirmed.

The code for scanning triplets is similar to that of scanning for twins. However, it is slightly more complex because now the application has to remember the coordinates of the three cells (the triplets) instead of just two cells (for twins). The coordinates of the three cells are saved as a string. For example, if the triplets are cells (1,1), (4,1), and (7,1), their coordinates will be saved as "114171".

Code the `LookForTripletsinMinigrids()` function as follows:

```
'============================================================
' Look for triplets in minigrids
'============================================================
Public Function LookForTripletsinMinigrids() As Boolean
    Dim changes As Boolean = False

    '---check each cell---
    For r As Integer = 1 To 9
        For c As Integer = 1 To 9

            '--- three possible values; check for triplets---
            If actual(c, r) = 0 AndAlso possible(c, r).Length = 3 Then

                '---first potential triplet found---
                Dim tripletsLocation As String = c.ToString() & r.ToString()

                '---scan by minigrid---
                Dim startC, startR As Integer
                startC = c - ((c - 1) Mod 3)
                startR = r - ((r - 1) Mod 3)

                For rr As Integer = startR To startR + 2
                    For cc As Integer = startC To startC + 2
```

```
            If (Not ((cc = c) AndAlso (rr = r))) AndAlso _
                ((possible(cc, rr) = possible(c, r)) OrElse _
                (possible(cc, rr).Length = 2 AndAlso _
                possible(c, r).Contains( _
                possible(cc, rr)(0).ToString()) AndAlso _
                possible(c, r).Contains( _
                possible(cc, rr)(1).ToString())))) Then

                '---save the coordinates of the triplets
                tripletsLocation &= cc.ToString() & rr.ToString()
            End If
        Next
    Next

    '--found 3 cells as triplets; remove all from the other
    ' cells---
    If tripletsLocation.Length = 6 Then

        '--triplets found---
        DisplayActivity("Triplets found in " & _
           tripletsLocation, False)

        '---remove each cell's possible values containing the
        ' triplet---
        For rrr As Integer = startR To startR + 2
            For ccc As Integer = startC To startC + 2

                '---look for the cell that is not part of the 3
                ' cells found---
                If actual(ccc, rrr) = 0 AndAlso _
                    ccc <> CInt(tripletsLocation(0).ToString()) _
                    AndAlso _
                    rrr <> CInt(tripletsLocation(1).ToString()) _
                    AndAlso _
                    ccc <> CInt(tripletsLocation(2).ToString()) _
                    AndAlso _
                    rrr <> CInt(tripletsLocation(3).ToString()) _
                    AndAlso _
                    ccc <> CInt(tripletsLocation(4).ToString()) _
                    AndAlso _
                    rrr <> CInt(tripletsLocation(5).ToString()) Then
```

```vb
'---save the original possible values---
Dim original_possible As String = _
   possible(ccc, rrr)
'---remove first triplet number from possible
' values---
possible(ccc, rrr) = _
   possible(ccc, rrr).Replace( _
   possible(c, r)(0), String.Empty)


'---remove second triplet number from possible
' values---
possible(ccc, rrr) = _
   possible(ccc, rrr).Replace( _
   possible(c, r)(1), String.Empty)


'---remove third triplet number from possible
' values---
possible(ccc, rrr) = _
   possible(ccc, rrr).Replace( _
   possible(c, r)(2), String.Empty)


'---set the ToolTip---
SetToolTip(ccc, rrr, possible(ccc, rrr))


'---if the possible values are modified, then
' set the changes variable to True to indicate
' that the possible values of cells in the
' minigrid have been modified---
If original_possible <> possible(ccc, rrr) Then
    changes = True
End If


'---if possible value reduces to empty string,
'then the user has placed a move that results
' in the puzzle being not solvable---
If possible(ccc, rrr) = String.Empty Then
    Throw New Exception("Invalid Move")
End If
```

```
                                    '---if left with 1 possible value for the
                                    ' current cell, cell is confirmed---
                                    If possible(ccc, rrr).Length = 1 Then
                                        SetCell(ccc, rrr, _
                                            CInt(possible(ccc, rrr)), 1)
                                        SetToolTip(ccc, rrr, possible(ccc, rrr))
                                        '---saves the move into the stack
                                        Moves.Push(ccc & rrr & possible(ccc, rrr))
                                        DisplayActivity( _
                                            "Look For Triplets in Minigrids)", _
                                            False)
                                        DisplayActivity( _
                                            "=============================", False)
                                        DisplayActivity( _
                                            "Inserted value " & actual(ccc, rrr) & _
                                            " in " & "(" & ccc & "," & rrr & ")", _
                                            False)
                                        Application.DoEvents()

                                        '---if user clicks the Hint button, exit
                                        ' the function---
                                        If HintMode Then Return True
                                    End If
                                End If
                            Next
                        Next
                    End If
                End If
            Next
        Next
        Return changes
    End Function
```

The LookForTripletsinMinigrids() function returns True if there are any changes to
the list of possible values for any of the cells in the grid. It returns False if none of the cells'
possible values is affected.

Looking for Triplets in Rows

The LookForTripletsinRows() function scans for triplets in each of the nine rows. It examines each row and scans its columns from left to right for triplets. As soon as it finds a cell
with three possible values, it scans starting from the next column until it reaches the last

column. If there is indeed a set of triplets in the row, the rest of the cells in the row will
have their list of possible values modified to eliminate the values of the triplets. After the
process, if there are cells left with one possible value, then those cells are confirmed.

Code the LookForTripletsinRows() function as follows:

```
'=============================================================
' Look for triplets in rows
'=============================================================
Public Function LookForTripletsinRows() As Boolean
    Dim changes As Boolean = False

    '---for each row, check each column in the row
    For r As Integer = 1 To 9
        For c As Integer = 1 To 9

            '--- three possible values; check for triplets---
            If actual(c, r) = 0 AndAlso possible(c, r).Length = 3 Then

                '---first potential triplet found---
                Dim tripletsLocation As String = c.ToString() & r.ToString()

                '--scans columns in this row---
                For cc As Integer = 1 To 9
                    '---look for other triplets---
                    If (cc <> c) AndAlso _
                      ((possible(cc, r) = possible(c, r)) OrElse _
                       (possible(cc, r).Length = 2 AndAlso _
                        possible(c, r).Contains( _
                        possible(cc, r)(0).ToString()) AndAlso _
                        possible(c, r).Contains( _
                        possible(cc, r)(1).ToString()))) Then
                        '---save the coordinates of the triplet---
                        tripletsLocation &= cc.ToString() & r.ToString()
                    End If
                Next

                '--found 3 cells as triplets; remove all from the other
                ' cells---
                If tripletsLocation.Length = 6 Then
```

```vbnet
                '--triplets found---
                DisplayActivity("Triplets found in " & tripletsLocation, _
                    False)

                '---remove each cell's possible values containing the
                ' triplet---
                For ccc As Integer = 1 To 9
                    If actual(ccc, r) = 0 AndAlso _
                        ccc <> CInt(tripletsLocation(0).ToString()) _
                        AndAlso _
                        ccc <> CInt(tripletsLocation(2).ToString()) _
                        AndAlso _
                        ccc <> CInt(tripletsLocation(4).ToString()) Then

                        '---save the original possible values---
                        Dim original_possible As String = possible(ccc, r)

                        '---remove first triplet number from possible
                        ' values---
                        possible(ccc, r) = _
                            possible(ccc, r).Replace(possible(c, r)(0), _
                            String.Empty)

                        '---remove second triplet number from possible
                        ' values---
                        possible(ccc, r) = _
                            possible(ccc, r).Replace(possible(c, r)(1), _
                            String.Empty)

                        '---remove third triplet number from possible
                        ' values---
                        possible(ccc, r) = _
                            possible(ccc, r).Replace(possible(c, r)(2), _
                            String.Empty)

                        '---set the ToolTip---
                        SetToolTip(ccc, r, possible(ccc, r))

                        '---if the possible values are modified, then set
                        ' the changes variable to True to indicate that the
                        ' possible values of cells in the minigrid have
                        ' been modified---
```

```vb
                If original_possible <> possible(ccc, r) Then
                    changes = True
                End If

                '---if possible value reduces to empty string, then
                ' the user has placed a move that results in the
                ' puzzle being not solvable---
                If possible(ccc, r) = String.Empty Then
                    Throw New Exception("Invalid Move")
                End If

                '---if left with 1 possible value for the current
                ' cell, cell is confirmed---
                If possible(ccc, r).Length = 1 Then
                    SetCell(ccc, r, CInt(possible(ccc, r)), 1)
                    SetToolTip(ccc, r, possible(ccc, r))

                    '---saves the move into the stack---
                    Moves.Push(ccc & r & possible(ccc, r))
                    DisplayActivity("Look For Triplets in Rows", _
                        False)
                    DisplayActivity("=========================", _
                        False)
                    DisplayActivity("Inserted value " & _
                        actual(ccc, r) & " in " & "(" & _
                        ccc & "," & r & ")", False)
                    Application.DoEvents()

                    '---if user clicks the Hint button, exit the
                    ' function---
                    If HintMode Then Return True
                End If
            End If
        Next
      End If
    End If
  Next
  Next
  Return changes
End Function
```

The LookForTripletsinRows() function returns True if there are any changes to the list of possible values for any of the cells in the grid. It returns False if none of the cells' possible values is affected.

Looking for Triplets in Columns

The LookForTripletsinColumns() function scans for triplets in each of the nine columns. It examines each column and scans its rows from top to bottom for triplets. As soon as it locates a cell with three possible values, it scans starting from the next row until it reaches the last row. If there is indeed a set of triplets in the column, the rest of the cells in the column will have their list of possible values modified to eliminate the values of the triplets. After the process, if there are cells left with one possible value, then those cells are confirmed.

Code the LookForTripletsinColumns() function as follows:

```
'===============================================================
' Look for triplets in columns
'===============================================================
Public Function LookForTripletsinColumns() As Boolean
    Dim changes As Boolean = False

    '---for each column, check each row in the column
    For c As Integer = 1 To 9
        For r As Integer = 1 To 9

            '--- three possible values; check for triplets---
            If actual(c, r) = 0 AndAlso possible(c, r).Length = 3 Then

                '---first potential triplet found---
                Dim tripletsLocation As String = c.ToString() & r.ToString()

                '--scans rows in this column---
                For rr As Integer = 1 To 9
                    If (rr <> r) AndAlso _
                        ((possible(c, rr) = possible(c, r)) OrElse _
                        (possible(c, rr).Length = 2 AndAlso _
                        possible(c, r).Contains( _
                        possible(c, rr)(0).ToString()) AndAlso _
                        possible(c, r).Contains( _
                        possible(c, rr)(1).ToString())))) Then
```

```vb
            '---save the coordinates of the triplet---
            tripletsLocation += c.ToString() & rr.ToString()
        End If
    Next

    '--found 3 cells as triplets; remove all from the other
    ' cells---
    If tripletsLocation.Length = 6 Then

        '--triplets found---
        DisplayActivity("Triplets found in " & tripletsLocation, _
            False)

        '---remove each cell's possible values containing the
        ' triplet---
        For rrr As Integer = 1 To 9
            If actual(c, rrr) = 0 AndAlso _
                rrr <> CInt(tripletsLocation(1).ToString()) _
                AndAlso _
                rrr <> CInt(tripletsLocation(3).ToString()) _
                AndAlso _
                rrr <> CInt(tripletsLocation(5).ToString()) Then

                '---save the original possible values---
                Dim original_possible As String = possible(c, rrr)

                '---remove first triplet number from possible
                ' values---
                possible(c, rrr) = _
                    possible(c, rrr).Replace( _
                    possible(c, r)(0), String.Empty)

                '---remove second triplet number from possible
                ' values---
                possible(c, rrr) = _
                    possible(c, rrr).Replace( _
                    possible(c, r)(1), String.Empty)
```

```vbnet
'---remove third triplet number from possible
' values---
possible(c, rrr) = _
   possible(c, rrr).Replace( _
   possible(c, r)(2), String.Empty)


'---set the ToolTip---
SetToolTip(c, rrr, possible(c, rrr))


'---if the possible values are modified, then set
' the changes variable to True to indicate that
' the possible values of cells in the minigrid
' have been modified---
If original_possible <> possible(c, rrr) Then
    changes = True
End If


'---if possible value reduces to empty string, then
' the user has placed a move that results in the
' puzzle being not solvable---
If possible(c, rrr) = String.Empty Then
    Throw New Exception("Invalid Move")
End If


'---if left with 1 possible value for the current
' cell, cell is confirmed---
If possible(c, rrr).Length = 1 Then
    SetCell(c, rrr, CInt(possible(c, rrr)), 1)
    SetToolTip(c, rrr, possible(c, rrr))

    '---saves the move into the stack
    Moves.Push(c & rrr & possible(c, rrr))
    DisplayActivity( _
       "Look For Triplets in Columns)", False)
    DisplayActivity( _
       "=============================", False)
    DisplayActivity( _
       "Inserted value " & actual(c, rrr) & _
       " in " & "(" & c & "," & rrr & ")", False)
    Application.DoEvents()
```

```
                                    '---if user clicks the Hint button, exit the
                                    ' function---
                                    If HintMode Then Return True
                                End If
                            End If
                    Next
                End If
            End If
        Next
    Next
    Return changes
End Function
```

The `LookForTripletsinColumns()` function returns `True` if there are any changes to the list of possible values for any of the cells in the grid. It returns `False` if none of the cells' possible values is affected.

Modifying the SolvePuzzle() Function

In the `SolvePuzzle()` function, add the following code in bold so that you now have a complete set of techniques to solve a Sudoku puzzle:

```
'==================================================
' Steps to solve the puzzle
'==================================================
Public Function SolvePuzzle() As Boolean
    Dim changes As Boolean
    Dim ExitLoop As Boolean = False
    Try
        Do '---Look for Triplets in Columns
            Do '---Look for Triplets in Rows
                Do '---Look for Triplets in Minigrids
                    Do '---Look for Twins in Columns
                        Do '---Look for Twins in Rows
                            Do '---Look for Twins in Minigrids
                                Do '---Look for Lone Ranger in Columns
                                    Do '---Look for Lone Ranger in Rows
                                        Do  '---Look for Lone Ranger in
                                            ' Minigrids
```

```
                              Do '---Perform Col/Row and
                                 ' Minigrid Elimination
                                 changes = _
                                     CheckColumnsAndRows()
                                 If (HintMode AndAlso changes) _
                                     OrElse IsPuzzleSolved() Then
                                         ExitLoop = True
                                         Exit Do
                                 End If
                              Loop Until Not changes

                              If ExitLoop Then Exit Do
                              '---Look for Lone Ranger in
                              ' Minigrids
                              changes = _
                                  LookForLoneRangersinMinigrids()
                              If (HintMode AndAlso changes) _
                                  OrElse IsPuzzleSolved() Then
                                      ExitLoop = True
                                      Exit Do
                              End If
                          Loop Until Not changes

                          If ExitLoop Then Exit Do
                          '---Look for Lone Ranger in Rows
                          changes = LookForLoneRangersinRows()
                          If (HintMode AndAlso changes) OrElse _
                              IsPuzzleSolved() Then
                                  ExitLoop = True
                                  Exit Do
                          End If
                      Loop Until Not changes

                      If ExitLoop Then Exit Do
                      '---Look for Lone Ranger in Columns
                      changes = LookForLoneRangersinColumns()
                      If (HintMode AndAlso changes) OrElse _
                          IsPuzzleSolved() Then
                              ExitLoop = True
                              Exit Do
                      End If
                  Loop Until Not changes
```

```
            If ExitLoop Then Exit Do
            '---Look for Twins in Minigrids
            changes = LookForTwinsinMinigrids()
            If (HintMode AndAlso changes) OrElse _
               IsPuzzleSolved() Then
                 ExitLoop = True
                 Exit Do
            End If
        Loop Until Not changes

        If ExitLoop Then Exit Do
        '---Look for Twins in Rows
        changes = LookForTwinsinRows()
        If (HintMode AndAlso changes) OrElse _
           IsPuzzleSolved() Then
             ExitLoop = True
             Exit Do
        End If
    Loop Until Not changes

    If ExitLoop Then Exit Do
    '---Look for Twins in Columns
    changes = LookForTwinsinColumns()
    If (HintMode AndAlso changes) OrElse _
       IsPuzzleSolved() Then
         ExitLoop = True
         Exit Do
    End If
Loop Until Not changes

If ExitLoop Then Exit Do
'---Look for Triplets in Minigrids
changes = LookForTripletsinMinigrids()
If (HintMode AndAlso changes) OrElse IsPuzzleSolved() Then
     ExitLoop = True
     Exit Do
End If
Loop Until Not changes
```

```
                    If ExitLoop Then Exit Do
                    '---Look for Triplets in Rows
                    changes = LookForTripletsinRows()
                    If (HintMode AndAlso changes) OrElse IsPuzzleSolved() Then
                        ExitLoop = True
                        Exit Do
                    End If
                Loop Until Not changes

                    If ExitLoop Then Exit Do
                    '---Look for Triplets in Columns
                    changes = LookForTripletsinColumns()
                    If (HintMode AndAlso changes) OrElse IsPuzzleSolved() Then
                        ExitLoop = True
                        Exit Do
                    End If
                Loop Until Not changes

        Catch ex As Exception
            Throw New Exception("Invalid Move")
        End Try

        If IsPuzzleSolved() Then
            Timer1.Enabled = False
            Beep()
            ToolStripStatusLabel1.Text = "*****Puzzle Solved*****"
            MsgBox("Puzzle solved")
            Return True
        Else
            Return False
        End If
    End Function
```

As you can probably deduce by now, at the inner core of the loop you first apply the CRME technique, followed by a search for lone rangers (in minigrids, rows, and columns), followed by a search for twins (in minigrids, rows, and columns), and finally by a search for triplets (in minigrids, rows, and columns). At the end of all the loops, if the puzzle is still not solved, then we have exhausted all logical means (at least the logical methods covered in this book) to solve the puzzle. At that point, we have to rely on some educated guesswork, as discussed in the next section.

Using Brute-Force Elimination

When all logical means have been used to solve a Sudoku puzzle and the puzzle remains unsolved, you have to perform some guesswork and choose a value for a cell and see if that helps to solve a puzzle. So let's now look at how you can implement the brute-force elimination technique in your code.

For the brute-force elimination technique, we need to add several member variables to the class:

```
Private BruteForceStop As Boolean = False
Private ActualStack As New Stack(Of Integer(,))()
Private PossibleStack As New Stack(Of String(,))()
```

The BruteForceStop Boolean variable is used to indicate if the brute-force method should stop (when the grid is solved). The ActualStack variable is a Stack object that is used to store the Actual array before a cell is fixed with a value. In the event that assigning a particular value to a cell causes the puzzle to have no solution, the Actual array is popped from the stack to restore the grid to its previous state. The PossibleStack variable is similar to the ActualStack variable, except that it is used to store the Possible array.

To find the cell with the least number of possible values, we will create the FindCellWithFewestPossibleValues() subroutine. It takes in two parameters passed in by reference. When the subroutine exits, the two parameters will contain the column and row number of the cell with the least number of possible values. The FindCellWithFewestPossibleValues() subroutine is defined as follows:

```
'===========================================================
' Find the cell with the least number of possible values
'===========================================================
Public Sub FindCellWithFewestPossibleValues( _
    ByRef col As Integer, ByRef row As Integer)
    Dim min As Integer = 10
    For r As Integer = 1 To 9
        For c As Integer = 1 To 9
            If actual(c, r) = 0 AndAlso possible(c, r).Length < min Then
                min = possible(c, r).Length
                col = c
                row = r
            End If
        Next
    Next
End Sub
```

Finally, the `SolvePuzzleByBruteForce()` subroutine is a recursive subroutine that attempts to solve a Sudoku puzzle by systematically selecting a possible value from a cell and then applying all the other technique to solve the puzzle. It calls itself until the puzzle is solved, or, if selecting a particular value for a cell causes the puzzle to be unsolvable, it backtracks by restoring the state of the grid using the two Stack objects, `ActualStack` and `PossibleStack`.

The code for the `SolvePuzzleByBruteForce()` subroutine is as follows:

```
'============================================================
' Brute Force subroutine
'============================================================
Public Sub SolvePuzzleByBruteForce()
    Dim c, r As Integer

    '---find out which cell has the smallest number of possible values---
    FindCellWithFewestPossibleValues(c, r)

    '---get the possible values for the chosen cell
    Dim possibleValues As String = possible(c, r)

    '---push the actual and possible stacks into the stack---
    ActualStack.Push(CType(actual.Clone(), Integer(,)))
    PossibleStack.Push(CType(possible.Clone(), String(,)))

    '---select one value and try---
    For i As Integer = 0 To possibleValues.Length - 1

        '---saves the move into the stack---
        Moves.Push(c & r & possibleValues(i).ToString())
        SetCell(c, r, CInt(possibleValues(i).ToString()), 1)
        DisplayActivity("Solve Puzzle By Brute Force", False)
        DisplayActivity("============================", False)
        DisplayActivity("Trying to insert value " & actual(c, r) & _
                        " in " & "(" & c & "," & r & ")", False)
    Try
        If SolvePuzzle() Then
            '---if the puzzle is solved, the recursion can stop now---
            BruteForceStop = True
            Return
```

```
            Else
                '---no problem with current selection, proceed with next cell---
                SolvePuzzleByBruteForce()
                If BruteForceStop Then Return
            End If
        Catch ex As Exception
            DisplayActivity("Invalid move; Backtracking...", False)
            actual = ActualStack.Pop()
            possible = PossibleStack.Pop()
        End Try
    Next
End Sub
```

If a number selected for a cell results in no solution for the puzzle, an exception will be raised. Handling this error is important, because it allows the subroutine to backtrack and restore the grid to its previous state and select another number to try. A good way to visualize how the subroutine works is to imagine solving the puzzle on paper. You select a number for a cell and check if you can derive the values for the other cells. If after a few tries you reach a dead end, you erase the last few cells that you have just filled in and select another number and try again.

Modifying the Code Behind for the Solve Puzzle Button

The last step we need to perform is to modify the code behind for the Solve Puzzle button so that if the puzzle cannot be solved using all the logical means, the application should then proceed to use the brute-force elimination technique.

```
'=====================================================
' Solve Puzzle button
'=====================================================
Private Sub btnSolvePuzzle_Click( _
    ByVal sender As System.Object, _
    ByVal e As System.EventArgs) _
    Handles btnSolvePuzzle.Click

    ActualStack.Clear()
    PossibleStack.Clear()
    BruteForceStop = False
    '---solve the puzzle; no need to stop---
    HintMode = False
```

```
        Try
            If Not SolvePuzzle() Then
                SolvePuzzleByBruteForce()
            End If
        Catch ex As Exception
            MsgBox("Puzzle not solvable.")
        End Try

        If Not IsPuzzleSolved() Then
            MsgBox("Puzzle Not solved.")
        End If

    End Sub
```

If you want to check if a puzzle can be solved logically without resorting to brute force, simply comment out the SolvePuzzleByBruteForce() function.

Testing the Techniques

With all the code in place, let's put all we have done into action and test a few puzzles. Figure 5-24 shows a Sudoku puzzle with 56 empty cells.

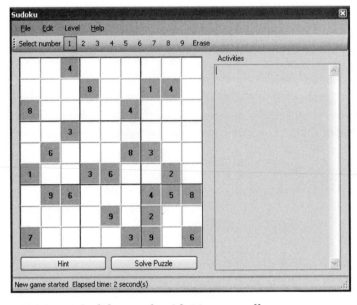

Figure 5-24. *A Sudoku puzzle with 56 empty cells*

Clicking the Solve Puzzle button solves the puzzle, fully exercising all the various techniques we have learned so far, as shown in Figure 5-25.

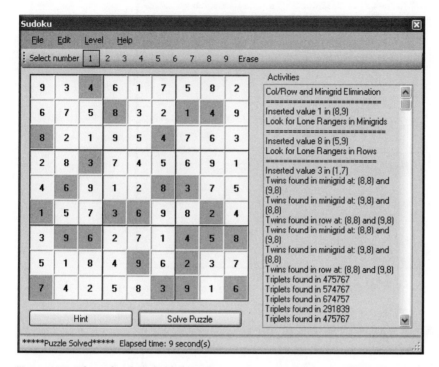

Figure 5-25. *The solved Sudoku puzzle!*

Note You may notice that when you click the Solve Puzzle button, the program seems to work pretty slowly, generating the numbers one by one. This is due not to the inefficiency of our techniques but rather to the large amount of text displayed in the TextBox control on the right of the grid. Try commenting out the two lines in the DisplayActivity() subroutine, and you will immediately notice how fast the program can solve the puzzle. In Chapter 6, you will get a better feel of how fast our techniques are.

What about another Sudoku puzzle? Figure 5-26 shows another example Sudoku puzzle.

Solving the puzzle requires using the brute-force technique only two times. The rest of the puzzle can be solved using the other techniques. Figure 5-27 shows the solution for this puzzle.

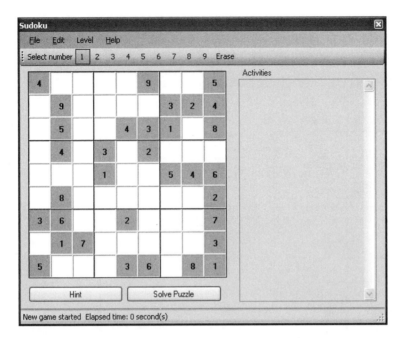

Figure 5-26. *Another Sudoku puzzle*

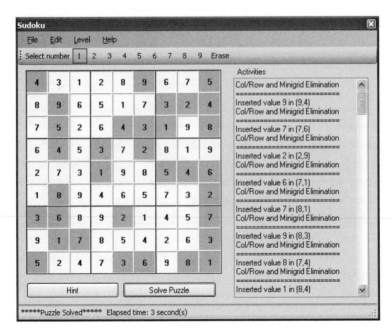

Figure 5-27. *The solved Sudoku puzzle*

What about "solving" an empty Sudoku puzzle? This will definitely require the brute-force elimination technique. To see if that works, execute the application and start a new puzzle (File ➤ New). Click Solve Puzzle to solve the puzzle (see Figure 5-28).

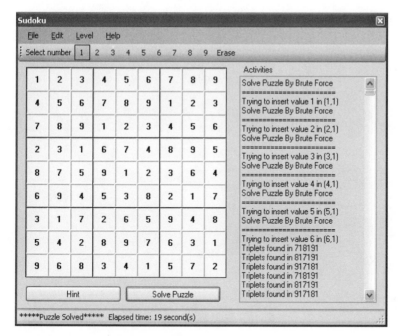

Figure 5-28. *Solving an empty Sudoku puzzle*

■Note It took about 19 seconds on my computer to "solve" the empty puzzle when I turned on display of the activities. Observe the messages displayed in the Activities textbox to see the different techniques used.

Notice that every time you solve an empty puzzle, you get the same solution. This is expected, because our implementation of the brute-force elimination technique systematically chooses the first possible number to try to solve the puzzle. If that fails, it goes on to select the next number. While in real life it is unlikely that you will be asked to solve an empty Sudoku puzzle, the ability to generate a valid Sudoku grid from scratch is important if you want to create new Sudoku puzzles. I will discuss this further in Chapter 6.

Summary

In this chapter, you have seen the three advanced techniques that you can use to solve Sudoku puzzles. Although most of the time twins and triplets will not directly solve the puzzle, they are good techniques for "softening" the puzzle so that the puzzle can be solved by other techniques such as CRME and lone rangers.

You have also seen how to use the brute-force technique to make an educated guess when all the other techniques have failed. In the next chapter, you will learn how to generate Sudoku puzzles of varying levels of difficulty.

■ ■ ■

CHAPTER 6

Generating Sudoku Puzzles

Yᵒu have come this far and have learned some very useful techniques for solving Sudoku puzzles. So far you have been learning how to solve puzzles; what about generating some new puzzles? There are a couple of good reasons for generating your own Sudoku puzzles. You may find that the puzzles you are currently solving are too simple and thus may want to generate some really tough puzzles to challenge yourself. Or you may want to test your friends by giving them some really tough puzzles and see them sweat. Or you may just be interested in learning how you can programmatically generate Sudoku puzzles. In this chapter, I will show you how to generate Sudoku puzzles of varying degrees of difficulty.

Determining the Level of Difficulty

To generate a Sudoku puzzle, you first need to consider the criteria for determining the level of difficulty of a Sudoku puzzle. The first factor that affects the difficulty is the number of empty cells in an initial Sudoku puzzle. In general, it is safe to say that the more empty cells you have in a Sudoku puzzle, the higher the level of difficulty. The second factor that affects the difficulty of a Sudoku puzzle is the placement of the various initial numbers. From observation, in general, simple puzzles often have their initial numbers evenly spaced apart, whereas difficult puzzles often have numbers clustered in groups. Evenly spaced cells can often be solved with CRME, because it performs best when rows, columns, and minigrids throughout the puzzle have a sufficient number of completed cells to effectively reduce the possible answers for individual cells.

■**Tip** Keep in mind that these are generalizations regarding the difficulty levels of puzzles; puzzles with initial numbers evenly spaced sometimes require some real effort to solve.

From a programming standpoint, we can determine the difficulty level of a Sudoku puzzle by analyzing how much effort must be expended to solve the puzzle. For the application that we are building in this book, I have set four levels of difficulty for Sudoku puzzles:

- Level 1 – Easy

- Level 2 – Medium

- Level 3 – Difficult

- Level 4 – Extremely Difficult

The level of difficulty for a puzzle will be determined by solving the puzzle using all the different techniques discussed in this book and examining how many times each technique is invoked to solve the puzzle. As discussed in the previous chapters, the following are techniques for solving a Sudoku puzzle:

- Column, Row, and Minigrid Elimination (CRME)

- Looking for lone rangers in minigrids/columns/rows

- Looking for twins in minigrids/columns/rows

- Looking for triplets in minigrids/columns/rows

- Brute-force elimination

As Sudoku puzzles get more complex, more advanced techniques are required to solve them, such as looking for twins and triplets, with the last resort being the brute-force elimination method. Relatively simple Sudoku puzzles can almost always be solved using the first two or three techniques.

To determine the difficulty level of a puzzle, we apply each of the preceding techniques in succession to try to solve the puzzle. Each time a cell is confirmed by a particular technique, we add points to a counter (the number of points we add depends on the technique applied). When the puzzle is solved, the total points accumulated serves as an indication of the total amount of effort needed to solve the puzzle. In general, the lower the points, the simpler the puzzle.

Table 6-1 lists the number of points I have designated for each technique.

Table 6-1. *Points Added for Each Technique*

Technique	Points
CRME	1
Lone rangers in minigrid	2
Lone rangers in column	2
Lone rangers in row	2
Twins in minigrid	3
Twins in column	3
Twins in row	3
Triplets in minigrid	4
Triplets in column	4
Triplets in row	4
Brute-force elimination	5
Backtracking in brute-force elimination	5

Based on the point system detailed in Table 6-1, every time we confirm a cell by using the CRME technique, we add 1 point, every time we confirm a cell by using the lone ranger method, we add 2 points, and so forth. In addition, if we have to backtrack because we have made a wrong decision, we also add 5 points, because this indicates that the puzzle contains cells with large numbers of possible values, which increases the possibility that the user will make a wrong decision. This situation is common for tough puzzles.

In general, most simple puzzles can be solved by using the first one or two techniques, so their total accumulated points should be significantly lower than that of more complex puzzles, which require more complex techniques to solve (and hence accumulate higher total points). In the next section, I outline the steps to generate Sudoku puzzles of various levels of difficulty.

Steps to Generate a Sudoku Puzzle

To generate a Sudoku puzzle, we start with an empty puzzle and use the brute-force approach to fill in all the empty cells. After we've done that, we judiciously remove some of the cells to give the user the starting point for their game. Our choice of how many cells to remove will depend on the level of difficulty the user specified. To ensure that you generate a different puzzle each time, you must randomize the list of possible values so that the brute-force technique has the chance to select different numbers in every pass.

■**Tip** Mathematically, you cannot guarantee that the puzzle generated is always new. But if you randomize the list of possible values, there is a high probability that every time you should get a different puzzle.

Once a complete grid is generated, it is now time to determine how many cells must be taken out (left empty). Based on my experience solving Sudoku puzzles, I have designated the number of empty cells for each level, as shown in Table 6-2.

Table 6-2. *Number of Empty Cells for Each Difficulty Level*

Level	Empty Cells
1 (Easy)	40 to 45
2 (Medium)	46 to 49
3 (Difficult)	50 to 53
4 (Extremely Difficult)	54 to 58

Once the actual number of empty cells is determined (the application randomly chooses a number within that range), the application randomly generates the locations of empty cells. For example, if you want to generate a level 2 Sudoku puzzle, you first determine how many empty cells are in the grid. Assuming the number is 47, you next proceed to determine the coordinates of 47 cells in the grid and set the value of these cells to 0.

■**Note** For this book, I am judging the level of difficulty of a Sudoku puzzle based on the number of empty cells in the puzzle and how much effort is needed to solve the puzzle. I will not consider the positioning of the empty cells as a factor affecting the difficulty level.

Once the empty cells are determined, you need to verify that the puzzle does indeed correspond to the level of difficulty indicated. To do this, you will solve the puzzle using all the techniques covered in this book and then examine its total score.

Based on empirical data derived through testing 10,000 Sudoku puzzles generated by my program, the average scores for the different levels are shown in Table 6-3.

Table 6-3. *Average Score for Each Difficulty Level*

Level	Empty Cells	Average Score
1	40 to 45	44
2	46 to 49	51
3	50 to 53	58
4	54 to 58	114

As you can see, the number of empty cells does have a direct impact on the score, which indicates the degree of difficulty.

When puzzles of specific levels of difficulty are generated, the application will test and compare the scores against the chart shown in Table 6-4. If the score does not fall into the respective range, the puzzle is regenerated and solved again. This process repeats until the score of the puzzle falls into the required range.

Table 6-4. *Acceptable Range of Points for Each Difficulty Level*

Level	Empty Cells	Average Score	Acceptable Range
1	40 to 45	44	42 to 46 inclusive
2	46 to 49	51	49 to 53 inclusive
3	50 to 53	58	56 to 60 inclusive
4	54 to 58	114	112 to 116 inclusive

Figure 6-1 summarizes the process to generate a Sudoku puzzle.

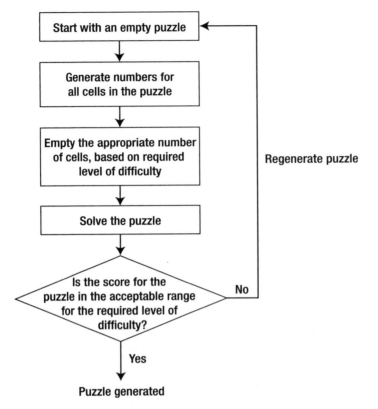

Figure 6-1. *Steps to generate a Sudoku puzzle*

Determining the Locations of Empty Cells

After an empty Sudoku puzzle is "solved," it is time to determine the locations of empty cells in the grid. Depending on the level of difficulty required, the number of empty cells is determined by the application. For example, if a level 1 puzzle is required, then a random number in the range of 40 to 45 is chosen. The next step would be to randomly choose the locations of the various empty cells.

Most of the published Sudoku puzzles are *symmetrical*. This means that the nonempty cells are distributed in rotationally symmetric cells. Consider the example shown in Figure 6-2.

Symmetrical Sudoku puzzles look pleasing to the eyes, though they are not strictly required. The puzzles that we will generate in this chapter are symmetrical. To ensure that a Sudoku puzzle is symmetrical, we first determine the locations of the empty cells in the top half of the puzzle, and then "mirror" them onto the bottom half.

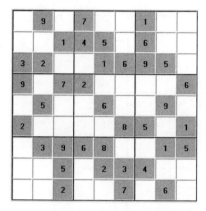

Figure 6-2. *A symmetrical Sudoku puzzle*

If the puzzle is rotated clockwise 180 degrees, the same cells are shaded, as shown in Figure 6-3.

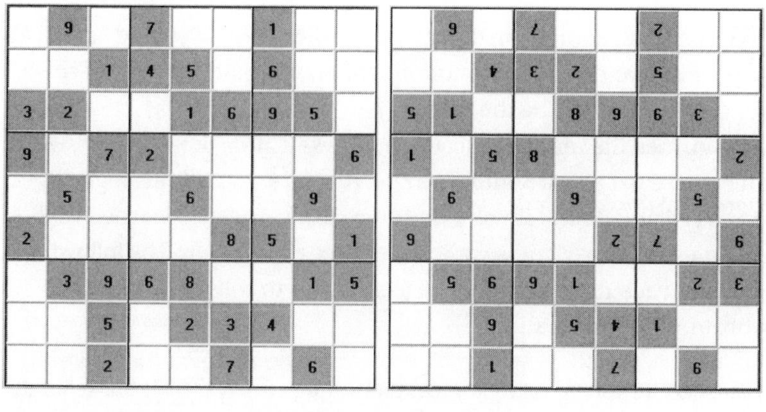

Figure 6-3. *Verifying that a Sudoku puzzle is symmetrical*

The shaded region on the left in Figure 6-4 shows the top half of the grid. Empty cells (determined randomly) are represented by ×. The top half of the grid is then rotated clockwise 180 degrees onto the bottom half of the grid so that the locations of the empty cells mirror the top half.

The end result of the rotation is a symmetrical Sudoku grid.

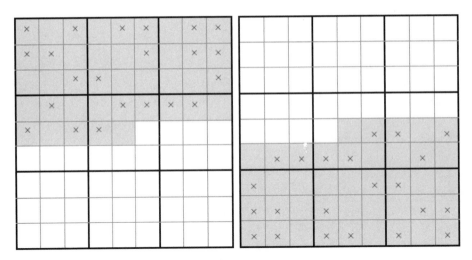

Figure 6-4. *Generating a symmetrical Sudoku grid in two steps*

Single-Solution Puzzles

In addition to being symmetrical, Sudoku puzzles have another, often-debated "rule": all Sudoku puzzles must have one and only one solution. That is, no matter how you solve the puzzle, the answer must ultimately be the same.

In Chapters 3 to 5, you learned the various logical techniques—CRME, lone rangers, twins, and triplets—that you can use to solve a Sudoku puzzle. All of these methods logically deduce the number for a cell and do not involve any guesswork. You also learned that when all else fails, you can use a form of guesswork, brute-force elimination. The following describes the difference between using only logical techniques to solve a puzzle and venturing into using brute-force elimination:

- If a Sudoku puzzle can be solved using logical techniques only, then it has a single solution.

- If a Sudoku puzzle requires some guesswork (that is, using the brute-force elimination technique) to solve, then the Sudoku puzzle is *not guaranteed* to have a single solution (that is, the puzzle has more than one correct solution).

The second point is interesting. Just because you apply the brute-force technique to solve a Sudoku puzzle does not necessarily mean that the puzzle does not have a single solution. It may still be a single-solution puzzle, but it may also have more than one solution, because there still might be some other logical means of solving the puzzle that we have not discovered yet.

For the puzzles that we will generate in this book, I have set the following guidelines:

- For levels 1 to 3, all puzzles are symmetrical and have a single solution.

- For level 4, all puzzles are symmetrical but there is no guarantee that they have a single solution. In other words, level 4 puzzles require some guesswork to solve.

For level 1 to 3 puzzles, once the empty cells in the grid are determined randomly by the application, you use all the logical techniques to solve it. If you cannot solve the puzzle, you randomly choose another pair of cells to vacate (you need to choose a pair of cells to vacate to ensure that the puzzle is symmetrical) and try to solve it logically again. You repeat this process a number of times until you either solve the puzzle or, if the puzzle is still unsolvable, generate a fresh new grid and repeat the entire process. Figure 6-5 summarizes the steps that you take to generate a level 1 to 3 puzzle.

For level 4 puzzles, once the grid is generated, you proceed to solve it using all the logical techniques. If it fails, the application uses the brute-force elimination technique to solve it. The overall score obtained will then be compared with the chart shown in Table 6-4. If its score falls outside the acceptable range, a fresh grid is generated and the entire process of solving and comparing the score is repeated.

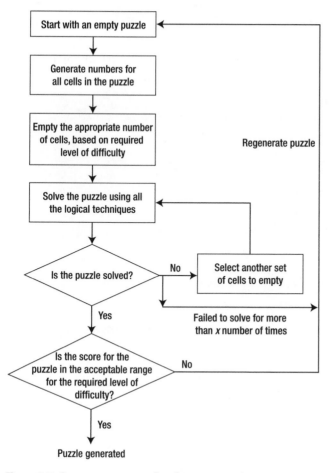

Figure 6-5. *Steps to generate level 1 to 3 puzzles*

Implementing the Puzzle-Generating Algorithm

To generate Sudoku puzzles, we use the same code base that we have built over the last few chapters. We package all the subroutines and functions that we have discussed into a class so that we have all the logic needed to solve and generate Sudoku puzzles.

■**Note** In the previous chapters, ideally, we would have had all the logic enclosed in a class, as we will in this chapter, so that regardless of whether we were solving or generating a Sudoku puzzle, we would have used the same code base. We did not enclose the logic in a class in those chapters because that would have made the code unnecessarily difficult to follow, especially with the injection of the various GUI code to display the activities. So, for the ease of explanation, in those chapters we had one code base for solving Sudoku puzzles. In this chapter, we have one code base both for solving and generating Sudoku puzzles, enclosed in a class.

Creating the Class

First, add a new class to the project by right-clicking the project name in Solution Explorer and selecting Add ➤ Class. Name the class **SudokuPuzzle.vb**. Solution Explorer should now look like Figure 6-6.

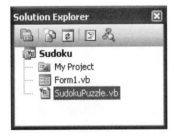

Figure 6-6. *The newly added SudokuPuzzle.vb class file*

Double-click the SudokuPuzzle.vb file and code the various functions and subroutines as shown in Listing 6-1.

■**Note** The complete code for Listing 6-1 appears as Listing A-1 in the Appendix.

Listing 6-1. *The SudokuPuzzle Class (Partial Content)*

```
Public Class SudokuPuzzle
    Private actual(9, 9) As Integer
    Private possible(9, 9) As String
    Private BruteForceStop As Boolean = False
    Private ActualStack As New Stack(Of Integer(,))()
    Private PossibleStack As New Stack(Of String(,))()

    '---store the total score accumulated---
    Private totalscore As Integer

    Private Function SolvePuzzle() As Boolean
    Private Function CheckColumnsAndRows() As Boolean
    Private Function CalculatePossibleValues( _
                    ByVal col As Integer, _
                    ByVal row As Integer) _
                    As String

    Private Function LookForLoneRangersinMinigrids() As Boolean
    Private Function LookForLoneRangersinRows() As Boolean
    Private Function LookForLoneRangersinColumns() As Boolean

    Private Function LookForTwinsinMinigrids() As Boolean
    Private Function LookForTwinsinRows() As Boolean
    Private Function LookForTwinsinColumns() As Boolean

    Private Function LookForTripletsinMinigrids() As Boolean
    Private Function LookForTripletsinRows() As Boolean
    Private Function LookForTripletsinColumns() As Boolean

    Private Sub FindCellWithFewestPossibleValues( _
        ByRef col As Integer, ByRef row As Integer)
    Private Sub SolvePuzzleByBruteForce()
    Private Function IsPuzzleSolved() As Boolean

End Class
```

Note the following about Listing 6-1:

- The code shown all comes from the previous few chapters, with the GUI code and comments stripped. See Listing A-1 for highlights of all the code changes.

- I have changed the access modifiers of all the functions and subroutines from Public to Private.

- A new member variable called totalscore is added. This variable is used to record the total score obtained when a puzzle is solved. The statements showing the accumulation of the score are shown in bold in each function (see Listing A-1 for all the locations to accumulate the total score).

The SudokuPuzzle class now contains all the code necessary to solve a Sudoku puzzle. We next add additional code so that we can use the class to generate Sudoku puzzles.

Randomizing the List of Possible Values

First, add the RandomizeThePossibleValues() subroutine to the SudokuPuzzle class. The RandomizeThePossibleValues() subroutine takes in a string parameter and randomly swaps the characters within the string. This subroutine is used to randomize the list of possible values for a cell.

The implementation of the RandomizeThePossibleValues() subroutine follows:

```
'===========================================================
' Randomly swap the list of possible values
'===========================================================
Private Sub RandomizeThePossibleValues(ByRef str As String)
    Dim s(str.Length - 1) As Char
    Dim i, j As Integer
    Dim temp As Char
    Randomize()
    s = str.ToCharArray
    For i = 0 To str.Length - 1
        j = CInt((str.Length - i + 1) * Rnd() + i) Mod str.Length
        '---swap the chars---
        temp = s(i)
        s(i) = s(j)
        s(j) = temp
    Next i
    str = s
End Sub
```

Modify the SolvePuzzleByBruteForce() subroutine so that the list of possible values for a cell is randomized before one of them is selected as a value for a cell:

```
'======================================================
' Solve puzzle by brute force
'======================================================
Private Sub SolvePuzzleByBruteForce()
    Dim c, r As Integer

    '---accumulate the total score---
    totalscore += 5

    FindCellWithFewestPossibleValues(c, r)
    Dim possibleValues As String = possible(c, r)

    '---randomize the possible values----
    RandomizeThePossibleValues(possibleValues)
    '-------------------

    ActualStack.Push(CType(actual.Clone(), Integer(,)))
    PossibleStack.Push(CType(possible.Clone(), String(,)))
    For i As Integer = 0 To possibleValues.Length - 1
        actual(c, r) = CInt(possibleValues(i).ToString())
        Try
            If SolvePuzzle() Then
                BruteForceStop = True
                Return
            Else
                SolvePuzzleByBruteForce()
                If BruteForceStop Then Return
            End If
        Catch ex As Exception
            '---accumulate the total score---
            totalscore += 5
            actual = ActualStack.Pop()
            possible = PossibleStack.Pop()
        End Try
    Next
End Sub
```

By randomizing the list of possible values for an empty cell, the SolvePuzzleByBruteForce() subroutine is now able to generate a fresh new grid whenever it is applied to an empty Sudoku puzzle.

Note There is one risk involved in randomizing the list of possible values. It may cause the program to go into a "flat spin" as the subroutine continues picking the same wrong number for each try. Mathematically, the chances are quite slim that the wrong number will always be selected, but it is still a remote possibility.

Generating a New Puzzle

The GenerateNewPuzzle() function generates a new Sudoku puzzle based on the level indicated in its first parameter and returns the score in its second parameter. It returns the new Sudoku puzzle as a string of numbers (in the same format as discussed in Chapter 1).

Code the GenerateNewPuzzle() function as follows:

```
'===============================================================
' Generate a new Sudoku puzzle
'===============================================================
Private Function GenerateNewPuzzle( _
    ByVal level As Integer, _
    ByRef score As Integer) As String

    Dim c, r As Integer
    Dim str As String
    Dim numberofemptycells As Integer

    '---initialize the entire board---
    For r = 1 To 9
        For c = 1 To 9
            actual(c, r) = 0
            possible(c, r) = String.Empty
        Next
    Next

    '---clear the stacks---
    ActualStack.Clear()
    PossibleStack.Clear()
```

```
'---populate the board with numbers by solving an empty grid---
Try
    '---use logical methods to set up the grid first---
    If Not SolvePuzzle() Then
        '---then use brute force---
        SolvePuzzleByBruteForce()
    End If
Catch ex As Exception
    '---just in case an error occurred, return an empty string---
    Return String.Empty
End Try

'---make a backup copy of the actual array---
actual_backup = actual.Clone()

'---set the number of empty cells based on the level of difficulty---
Select Case level
    Case 1 : numberofemptycells = RandomNumber(40, 45)
    Case 2 : numberofemptycells = RandomNumber(46, 49)
    Case 3 : numberofemptycells = RandomNumber(50, 53)
    Case 4 : numberofemptycells = RandomNumber(54, 58)
End Select

'---clear the stacks that are used in brute-force elimination ---
ActualStack.Clear()
PossibleStack.Clear()
BruteForceStop = False

'----create empty cells----
CreateEmptyCells(numberofemptycells)

'---convert the values in the actual array to a string---
str = String.Empty
For r = 1 To 9
    For c = 1 To 9
        str &= actual(c, r).ToString()
    Next
Next
```

```vbnet
        '---verify the puzzle has only one solution---
        Dim tries As Integer = 0
        Do
            totalscore = 0
            Try
                If Not SolvePuzzle() Then
                    '---if puzzle is not solved and
                    ' this is a level 1 to 3 puzzle---
                    If level < 4 Then
                        '---choose another pair of cells to empty---
                        VacateAnotherPairOfCells(str)
                        tries += 1
                    Else
                        '---level 4 puzzles do not guarantee single
                        ' solution and potentially need guessing---
                        SolvePuzzleByBruteForce()
                        Exit Do
                    End If
                Else
                    '---puzzle does indeed have 1 solution---
                    Exit Do
                End If
            Catch ex As Exception
                Return String.Empty
            End Try

            '---if too many tries, exit the loop---
            If tries > 50 Then
                Return String.Empty
            End If
        Loop While True
        '==================================================

        '---return the score as well as the puzzle as a string---
        score = totalscore
        Return str
    End Function
```

As you can observe from the preceding code, you first solve an empty puzzle by applying the SolvePuzzle() function. This function prepares the grid by generating all the possible values for the empty cells. Obviously, at this stage it is not possible to solve the empty grid using logic alone; hence, you have to apply the SolvePuzzleByBruteForce() subroutine to solve it:

```
'---populate the board with numbers by solving an empty grid---
Try
    '---use logical methods to set up the grid first---
    If Not SolvePuzzle() Then
        '---then use brute force---
        SolvePuzzleByBruteForce()
    End If
Catch ex As Exception
    '---just in case an error occurred, return an empty string---
    Return String.Empty
End Try
```

Once a grid is filled with numbers, you will randomly choose the number of empty cells based on the level desired. The CreateEmptyCells() subroutine is called to randomly remove cells from the grid (discussed further in the next section).

Once the empty cells are determined, you will save the puzzle as a string and then proceed to solve the puzzle. For a level 1 to 3 puzzle, you must ensure that it has only one solution, and hence you need to solve the puzzle logically without resorting to brute force. If you cannot solve the puzzle logically, you will choose another set of cells to empty and try again (achieved by calling the VacateAnotherPairOfCells() subroutine, which I will discuss later) until the puzzle is solved. This process is repeated up to 50 times, after which the entire grid is aborted and the GenerateNewPuzzle() function returns an empty string, signaling its failure to generate a puzzle of the desired difficulty level. For level 4 puzzles, the process is straightforward—solve the puzzle using logical techniques and brute force (if needed) and return the puzzle as a string.

■**Note** The reason why you need to solve a puzzle immediately after it is generated is that you need to determine the score that is used up to solve the puzzle. This ensures that puzzles are of the right level of difficulty.

The GenerateNewPuzzle() function made several calls to the RandomNumber() function, which returns a random number between the two specified parameters. Add the RandomNumber() function to the class as follows:

```
'=============================================================
' Generate a random number between the specified range
'=============================================================
Private Function RandomNumber(ByVal min As Integer, _
                     ByVal max As Integer) As Integer
    Return Int((max - min + 1) * Rnd()) + min
End Function
```

The minimum and maximum numbers are inclusive of the lower and upper bounds. That is, RandomNumber(1,9) generates a random number from 1 to 9, inclusive.

Creating Empty Cells in the Grid

The CreateEmptyCells() subroutine randomly determines the location of empty cells in the Sudoku grid. It first generates the location of empty cells in the top half of the grid (as described in conjunction with Figure 6-4, earlier). It then "reflects" the empty cells onto the bottom half of the grid so that a symmetrical Sudoku puzzle is achieved.

The implementation of the CreateEmptyCells() subroutine is as follows:

```
'=============================================================
'  Create empty cells in the grid
'=============================================================
Private Sub CreateEmptyCells(ByVal empty As Integer)
    Dim c, r As Integer
    '----choose random locations for empty cells----
    Dim emptyCells(empty - 1) As String
    For i As Integer = 0 To (empty \ 2)
        Dim duplicate As Boolean
        Do
            duplicate = False
            '---get a cell in the first half of the grid
            Do
                c = RandomNumber(1, 9)
                r = RandomNumber(1, 5)
            Loop While (r = 5 And c > 5)
```

```
For j As Integer = 0 To i
    '---if cell is already selected to be empty
    If emptyCells(j) = c.ToString() & r.ToString() Then
        duplicate = True
        Exit For
    End If
Next

If Not duplicate Then
    '---set the empty cell---
    emptyCells(i) = c.ToString() & r.ToString()
    actual(c, r) = 0
    possible(c, r) = String.Empty

    '---reflect the top half of the grid and make it symmetrical---
    emptyCells(empty - 1 - i) = _
        (10 - c).ToString() & (10 - r).ToString()
    actual(10 - c, 10 - r) = 0
    possible(10 - c, 10 - r) = String.Empty
End If
    Loop While duplicate
    Next
End Sub
```

The locations of empty cells are stored in an array. For example, if there are 48 empty cells, then the emptyCells() array has 48 members, with indices from 0 to 47. The location of each empty cell is stored as a string. Figure 6-7 shows how the empty cells are represented in the array.

emptyCells (0)	11	Cell (1,1) is empty
emptyCells (1)	31	Cell (3,1) is empty
emptyCells (2)	25	Cell (2,5) is empty
...	..	
...	..	
emptyCells (45)	85	Cell (8,5) is empty, symmetrical reflection of (2,5)
emptyCells (46)	79	Cell (7,9) is empty, symmetrical reflection of (3,1)
emptyCells (47)	99	Cell (9,9) is empty, symmetrical reflection of (1,1)

Figure 6-7. *Representing the locations of empty cells in an array*

Finding the location of symmetrical cells is surprisingly easy. Consider the grid shown in Figure 6-8. The grid contains two pairs of symmetrical cells. Cell (2,1)'s symmetrical counterpart is (8,9), and cell (1,4)'s symmetrical counterpart is (9,6). If you examine the coordinates of these cells closely, you will discover that both their row and column indices add up to 10.

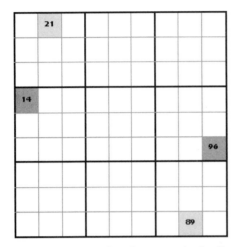

Figure 6-8. *Two pairs of symmetrical cells*

For example, the sum of the columns of (2,1) and (8,9) is 10 (2 + 8). Likewise, the sum of their rows is also 10 (1 + 9). You can verify this principle for the other pair of cells. So, given the coordinate of a cell (*c*,*r*), its symmetrical counterpart is (10 – *c*,10 – *r*).

Vacating Another Pair of Cells

For a level 1 to 3 puzzle, you ensure that it has one solution by enforcing that the puzzles be solved logically. If the puzzle cannot be solved logically, a feasible remedy would be to restore the value for a random pair of cells and re-determine another set of empty cells and see if that enables the puzzle to be solved. This task is accomplished by the VacateAnotherPairOfCells() subroutine.

The implementation of the VacateAnotherPairOfCells() subroutine is as follows:

```
'================================================================
' Vacate another pair of cells
'================================================================
Private Sub VacateAnotherPairOfCells(ByRef str As String)
    Dim c, r As Integer

    '---look for a pair of cells to restore---
    Do
        c = RandomNumber(1, 9)
        r = RandomNumber(1, 9)
```

```
    Loop Until str((c - 1) + (r - 1) * 9).ToString() = 0

    '---restore the value of the cell from the actual_backup array---
    str = str.Remove((c - 1) + (r - 1) * 9, 1)
    str = str.Insert((c - 1) + (r - 1) * 9, _
        actual_backup(c, r).ToString())

    '---restore the value of the symmetrical cell from
    ' the actual_backup array---
    str = str.Remove((10 - c - 1) + (10 - r - 1) * 9, 1)
    str = str.Insert((10 - c - 1) + (10 - r - 1) * 9, _
        actual_backup(10 - c, 10 - r).ToString())

    '---look for another pair of cells to vacate---
    Do
        c = RandomNumber(1, 9)
        r = RandomNumber(1, 9)
    Loop Until str((c - 1) + (r - 1) * 9).ToString() <> 0

    '---remove the cell from the str---
    str = str.Remove((c - 1) + (r - 1) * 9, 1)
    str = str.Insert((c - 1) + (r - 1) * 9, "0")

    '---remove the symmetrical cell from the str---
    str = str.Remove((10 - c - 1) + (10 - r - 1) * 9, 1)
    str = str.Insert((10 - c - 1) + (10 - r - 1) * 9, "0")

    '---reinitialize the board---
    Dim counter As Short = 0
    For row As Integer = 1 To 9
        For col As Integer = 1 To 9
            If CInt(str(counter).ToString()) <> 0 Then
                actual(col, row) = CInt(str(counter).ToString())
                possible(col, row) = str(counter).ToString()
            Else
                actual(col, row) = 0
                possible(col, row) = String.Empty
            End If
            counter += 1
        Next
    Next
End Sub
```

In the VacateAnotherPairOfCells() subroutine, you need to directly manipulate the
str (representing the puzzle) variable when restoring and emptying a new pair of cells.
You cannot directly modify the actual() array, because during the time when this subroutine
is called, the actual() array would contain the partially solved puzzle, and modifying the
actual() array at this stage would mess up the puzzle. Instead, you need to manipulate
the original puzzle as represented by the str variable. To restore a pair of cells, you simply
get the original values of the pair from the actual_backup() array.

Figure 6-9 shows how to translate the location of a cell in a grid to the index in a string
variable.

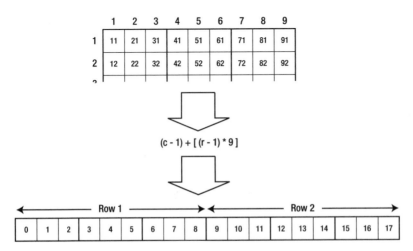

Figure 6-9. *Translating the address from a cell to a string variable*

Once the pair of cells has been restored and a new pair of empty cells inserted, you can
reinitialize the board by resetting the actual() and possible() arrays from the str variable.

Exposing the GetPuzzle() Function

With all the logic for generating new Sudoku puzzles defined, it is finally time for us to
expose the GetPuzzle() function so that the Sudoku application can call it to obtain a new
puzzle.

The GetPuzzle() function calls the GenerateNewPuzzle() function and ensures that the
puzzle is of the right level of difficulty. It does so by checking the score of the puzzle and
then generating a new puzzle if the score does not match the level of difficulty required:

```
'===============================================================
' Get Puzzle
'===============================================================
Public Function GetPuzzle(ByVal level As Integer) As String
    Dim score As Integer
```

```
    Dim result As String
    Do
        result = GenerateNewPuzzle(level, score)
        If result <> String.Empty Then
            '---check if puzzle matches the level of difficulty---
            Select Case level
                '---average for this level is 44---
                Case 1 :
                    If score >= 42 And score <= 46 Then
                        Exit Do
                    End If
                    '---average for this level is 51---
                Case 2 :
                    If score >= 49 And score <= 53 Then
                        Exit Do
                    End If
                    '---average for this level is 58---
                Case 3 :
                    If score >= 56 And score <= 60 Then
                        Exit Do
                    End If
                    '---average for this level is 114---
                Case 4 :
                    If score >= 112 And score <= 116 Then
                        Exit Do
                    End If
            End Select
        End If
    Loop Until False
    Return result
End Function
```

During the testing of the application, generating a level 3 puzzle takes a little longer than generating puzzles of the other levels, because level 3 puzzles have more empty cells and require more tries to solve by all the logical methods (since they must have a single solution). In contrast, level 4 puzzles take less time to generate because there is no need to ensure that they have a single solution. In general, level 1 puzzles take the least time to generate, followed by level 2, and then level 3 puzzles. The time needed to generate level 4 puzzles sometimes is as long as level 1 and 2 puzzles, because additional time is used for brute-force elimination (and possibly lots of backtracking).

Wiring Up the Logic with the User Interface

Now that we have all the code to generate new Sudoku puzzles, let's wire up all the logic with the GUI portion of the application.

Recall from Chapter 2 that the Level menu has four menu items: Easy, Medium, Difficult, and Extremely Difficult (see Figure 6-10). Using this menu, users can select the level of difficulty for each Sudoku puzzle. When the user selects a level, we display a checkmark next to the menu item. To do so, set the CheckOnClick property of each menu item to True, as shown in Figure 6-10.

■**Tip** You can set the CheckOnClick property for all menu items simultaneously in the Designer by holding down the Control key and clicking each menu item, and then modifying the CheckOnClick property in the Properties window.

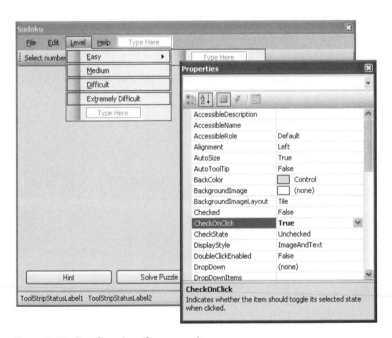

Figure 6-10. *Configuring the menu items*

Also, set the Checked property of the Easy menu item to True so that the default level is always Easy.

Double-click each menu item to switch to its code behind and code the following:

```
Private Sub EasyToolStripMenuItem_Click( _
   ByVal sender As System.Object, ByVal e As System.EventArgs) _
   Handles EasyToolStripMenuItem.Click
     MediumToolStripMenuItem.Checked = False
     DifficultToolStripMenuItem.Checked = False
     ExtremelyDifficultToolStripMenuItem.Checked = False
End Sub

Private Sub MediumToolStripMenuItem_Click( _
   ByVal sender As System.Object, ByVal e As System.EventArgs) _
   Handles MediumToolStripMenuItem.Click
     EasyToolStripMenuItem.Checked = False
     DifficultToolStripMenuItem.Checked = False
     ExtremelyDifficultToolStripMenuItem.Checked = False
End Sub

Private Sub DifficultToolStripMenuItem_Click( _
   ByVal sender As System.Object, ByVal e As System.EventArgs) _
   Handles DifficultToolStripMenuItem.Click
     EasyToolStripMenuItem.Checked = False
     MediumToolStripMenuItem.Checked = False
     ExtremelyDifficultToolStripMenuItem.Checked = False
End Sub

Private Sub ExtremelyDifficultToolStripMenuItem_Click( _
   ByVal sender As System.Object, ByVal e As System.EventArgs) _
   Handles ExtremelyDifficultToolStripMenuItem.Click
     EasyToolStripMenuItem.Checked = False
     MediumToolStripMenuItem.Checked = False
     DifficultToolStripMenuItem.Checked = False
End Sub
```

Once you do this, the next time a user selects a level, she will be able to see the check-mark next to the selected level, as shown in Figure 6-11.

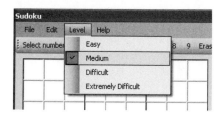

Figure 6-11. *Displaying a checkmark next to the selected menu item*

To generate a new puzzle and load it onto the grid when the user selects File ➤ New, double-click the File ➤ New menu item and modify its code behind as follows:

```
'=================================================
' Start a new game
'=================================================
Private Sub NewToolStripMenuItem_Click( _
    ByVal sender As System.Object, _
    ByVal e As System.EventArgs) _
    Handles NewToolStripMenuItem.Click

    If GameStarted Then
        Dim response As MsgBoxResult = _
            MessageBox.Show("Do you want to save current game?", _
                            "Save current game", _
                            MessageBoxButtons.YesNoCancel, _
                            MessageBoxIcon.Question)

        If response = MsgBoxResult.Yes Then
            SaveGameToDisk(False)
        ElseIf response = MsgBoxResult.Cancel Then
            Return
        End If
    End If

    '---change to the hourglass cursor---
    Windows.Forms.Cursor.Current = Cursors.WaitCursor
    ToolStripStatusLabel1.Text = "Generating new puzzle..."

    '---create an instance of the SudokuPuzzle class---
    Dim sp As New SudokuPuzzle
    Dim puzzle As String = String.Empty

    '---determine the correct level---
    If EasyToolStripMenuItem.Checked Then
        puzzle = sp.GetPuzzle(1)
    ElseIf MediumToolStripMenuItem.Checked Then
        puzzle = sp.GetPuzzle(2)
```

```
    ElseIf DifficultToolStripMenuItem.Checked Then
        puzzle = sp.GetPuzzle(3)
    ElseIf ExtremelyDifficultToolStripMenuItem.Checked Then
        puzzle = sp.GetPuzzle(4)
    End If

    '---change back to the default cursor
    Windows.Forms.Cursor.Current = Cursors.Default

    StartNewGame()

    '---initialize the board---
    Dim counter As Integer = 0
    For row As Integer = 1 To 9
        For col As Integer = 1 To 9

            If puzzle(counter).ToString() <> "0" Then
                SetCell(col, row, CInt(puzzle(counter).ToString()), 0)
            End If
            counter += 1
        Next
    Next
End Sub
```

Essentially, you create an instance of the SudokuPuzzle class and then invoke the GetPuzzle() method to generate a new Sudoku puzzle. While the puzzle is being generated, you display an hourglass icon to indicate to the user that the application is busy. Once the new puzzle is ready, it is loaded onto the board.

Testing the Implementation

We can now test the fruit of our labor. Let's generate a series of puzzles of different levels of difficulty and see if you can solve them. Have fun!

Easy Puzzles

Figure 6-12 shows a puzzle rated as Easy.

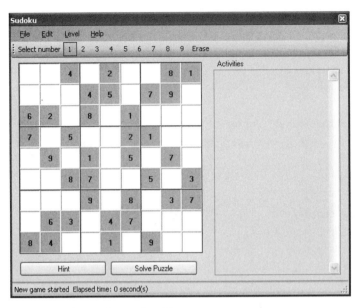

Figure 6-12. *A puzzle rated as Easy*

Clicking the Solve Puzzle button solves the puzzle. Figure 6-13 shows the solution for the puzzle.

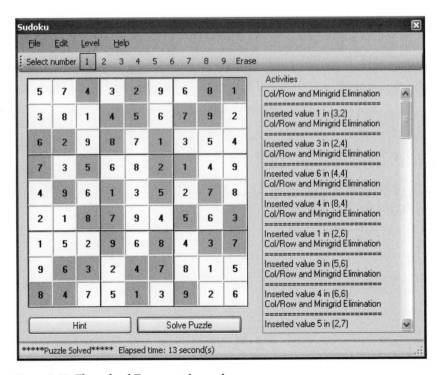

Figure 6-13. *The solved Easy-rated puzzle*

Medium Puzzles

Figure 6-14 shows a puzzle rated as Medium.

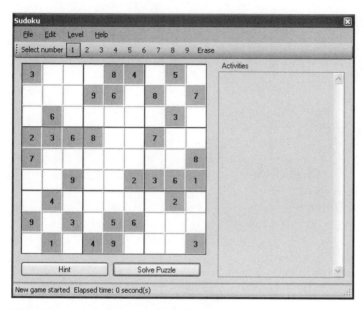

Figure 6-14. *A puzzle rated as Medium*

Figure 6-15 shows its solution.

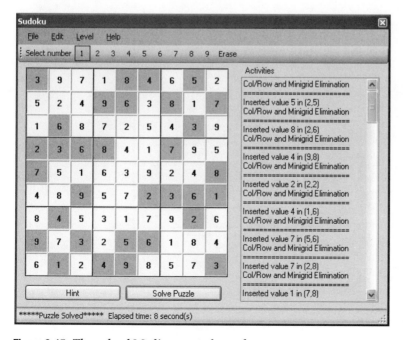

Figure 6-15. *The solved Medium-rated puzzle*

Difficult Puzzles

Figure 6-16 shows a puzzle rated as Difficult.

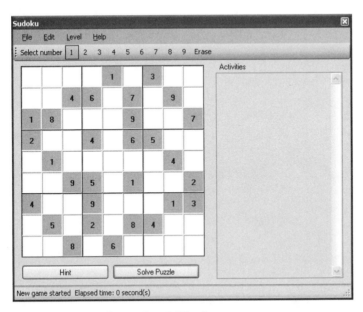

Figure 6-16. *A puzzle rated as Difficult*

Figure 6-17 shows its solution.

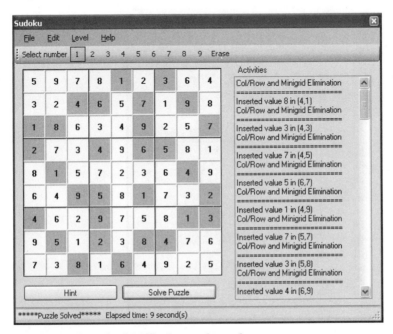

Figure 6-17. *The solved Difficult-rated puzzle*

Extremely Difficult Puzzles

Figure 6-18 shows a puzzle rated as Extremely Difficult.

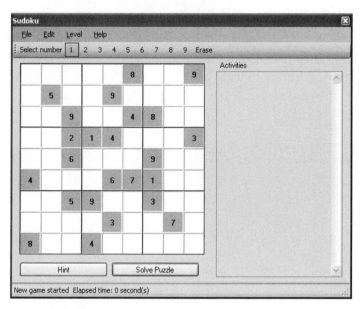

Figure 6-18. *A puzzle rated as Extremely Difficult*

Figure 6-19 shows its solution.

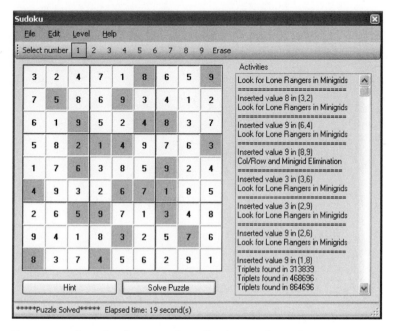

Figure 6-19. *The solved Extremely Difficult–rated puzzle*

Summary

This chapter combines all the techniques that you have learned in the past few chapters and uses them to generate Sudoku puzzles of varying levels of difficulty. While I have described the techniques to generate Sudoku puzzles, you can adapt the methods to further improve the quality of the puzzles. In fact, there are many areas of improvements that you might want to look into, such as adjusting the weights assigned to each technique that is used to solve a puzzle to further fine-tune the difficulty levels. Also, you can insert additional checks in the program so that the puzzles generated can have only one solution.

CHAPTER 7

■■■

How to Play Kakuro

As the book goes to press, Kakuro, a numbers-based puzzle game similar to Sudoku, is quickly gaining popularity. Like Sudoku, Kakuro puzzles use the numbers 1 to 9 and provide hours of fun and challenges. Think of Kakuro as the numerical equivalent of crossword puzzles. Instead of filling in the crossword puzzle with letters, you fill it in with numbers. In this chapter, I show you how to play Kakuro and share some tips for solving Kakuro puzzles. Although I won't show you the programmatic steps to solve a Kakuro puzzle, you can apply the logical techniques used to solve Sudoku puzzles to solve Kakuro puzzles as well.

The Rules

A typical Kakuro puzzle looks like Figure 7-1.

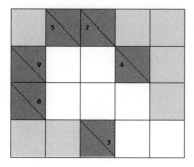

Figure 7-1. *A Kakuro puzzle*

Like Sudoku, Kakuro puzzles are not fixed in size. A Kakuro puzzle contains a number of empty cells as well as bisected cells with numbers in them, known as *clue squares*. Using the puzzle shown in Figure 7-1, the boxed cells shown in Figure 7-2 are the clue squares.

■**Note** For easier referencing, I will refer to each individual cell in a Kakuro puzzle by its column and row number, as I did for the Sudoku puzzles' cells.

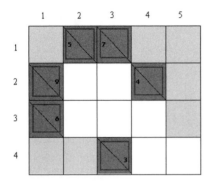

Figure 7-2. *Clue squares in a Kakuro puzzle*

■**Note** The empty shaded cells are not in use; they are like the black squares in a crossword puzzle.

Each clue square contains one or two numbers. Figure 7-3 shows an example of an "across" clue (borrowing crossword puzzle terminology). The 6 in the top-right corner of the cell is the clue for the row. It indicates that the values of the next consecutive series of empty cells must all add up to 6, with the following restrictions:

- Each cell must be filled with a number from 1 to 9.

- Cells in a row (or column) cannot have repeating numbers.

Figure 7-3. *An example of an across clue*

Figure 7-4 shows a likely combination of values for the three cells. Other combinations are also possible, like 2,1,3 or 3,1,2. Combinations like 1,1,4 and 2,2,2 are invalid because they contain duplicates.

Figure 7-4. *Possible values for the three cells*

Besides across clues, there are "down" clues (again using crossword puzzle terminology). An example is shown in Figure 7-5. The number written in the bottom-left corner of the cell is the clue for the column.

Figure 7-5. *A down clue*

Here, the values for the two cells highlighted in Figure 7-5 must add up to 7. Possible combinations are 1,6, 2,5, and 3,4.

■**Note** Clue squares can also contain both across and down clues. In such cases, there are two numbers in the clue square—one in the top-right corner and the other in the bottom-left corner.

The objective of the game is to fill up the grid with numbers so that each cell contains a number that fulfills the across and down rules. Sounds easy? Let's try to solve a Kakuro puzzle.

Solving a Kakuro Puzzle

Now that you have seen what a Kakuro puzzle looks like and learned the rules, it is time to solve one yourself. I will walk you through the process of solving a simple Kakuro puzzle, using the same puzzle shown earlier.

First, consider the two boxed cells highlighted in the bottom-right corner of Figure 7-6.

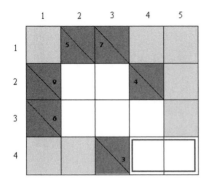

Figure 7-6. *Considering a set of two cells in a row*

The two cells can take the value of 1,2 or 2,1. However, if you consider two vertical cells (see Figure 7-7), the possible values for these cells are 1,3 or 3,1. They cannot have the values 2,2, since this violates the rules of Kakuro. Furthermore, cell (4,4) cannot take the value 3, since that leaves (5,4) with no allowable values (remember that cells (4,4) and (5,4) must add up to 3). Hence, that leaves only one possible value for cell (4,4), which is 1.

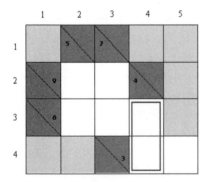

Figure 7-7. *Considering a set of two cells in a column*

With (4,4) confirmed with the number 1, it is now easy to fill in the numbers for (4,3) and (5,4), as shown in Figure 7-8.

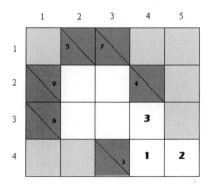

Figure 7-8. *Filling in the cells (4,3) and (5,4)*

We are now left with four cells. Let's start with the smallest clue number to add up to. It's always a good idea to start with the smallest clue number to add up to, because there are fewer possible combinations that fit the clue. If you look at the current grid, the smallest clue number to add up to is not 5 (cell (2,1)), but 6 (cell (1,3)), because effectively for cell (1,3), 3 out of a total of 6 is already taken up, by cell (4,3). Thus, we now need to consider only the two boxed cells shown in Figure 7-9.

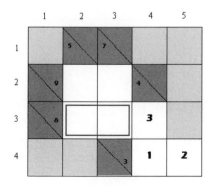

Figure 7-9. *Considering two cells instead of three*

The possible values for these two cells are 1,2 and 2,1. Since the number of cells left is quite small and filling in the two cells with 1,2 or 2,1 does not cause problems for other cells, let's try to fill in the two cells with 1,2, as shown in Figure 7-10.

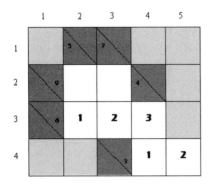

Figure 7-10. *Filling in the two cells*

Now see if you can complete the grid. In fact, you can solve the puzzle, by filling in (2,2) with 4 and (3,2) with 5, as shown in Figure 7-11.

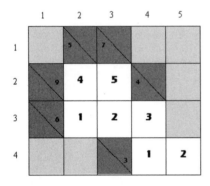

Figure 7-11. *Solving the puzzle*

Interestingly, this Kakuro puzzle has more than one solution. If you instead choose 2,1 for the two cells (2,3) and (3,3), you get a different solution (see Figure 7-12).

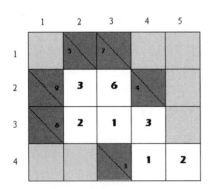

Figure 7-12. *Multiple-solution puzzle*

■**Note** There are no hard and fast rules stating that a Kakuro puzzle must have a unique solution. Some web sites, however, insist that a good Kakuro puzzle must have only one solution. I will leave that judgment to you.

Tips for Solving Kakuro Puzzles

If you have followed the previous section closely, you should be able to observe that knowing the composition of a number is one of the keys to solving Kakuro puzzles. For example, the number 6 is made up of 1, 2, and 3. You can also think of it as made up of 2 and 4, or 1 and 5. Having a table that lists all the possible combinations is useful. Table 7-1 shows a partial list of such numbers.

Table 7-1. *Composition of Numbers for Various Number of Cells*

Number of Cells	Number	Composition
2	3	1 2
	4	1 3
	5	1 4
		2 3
	6	1 5
		2 4
	7	1 6
		2 5
		3 4
	8	1 7
		2 6
		3 5
3	6	1 2 3
	7	1 2 4
	8	1 2 5
		1 3 4
	9	1 2 6
		1 3 5
		2 3 4
4	10	1 2 3 4
	11	1 2 3 5

Table 7-1. *Composition of Numbers for Various Number of Cells (Continued)*

Number of Cells	Number	Composition
	12	1 2 3 6
		1 2 4 5
	13	1 2 3 7
		1 2 4 6
		1 3 4 5
5	15	1 2 3 4 5
	16	1 2 3 4 6
	17	1 2 3 4 7
		1 2 3 5 6

In addition, it is always easier to start with the clue that has the smallest number to add up to. Working with the smallest number often allows other clues to be reduced and subsequently solved. In our earlier example, confirming a cell with the value 3 effectively reduces the across clue value of 6 to 3, since 3 is already filled in the third cell (see Figure 7-13).

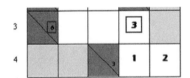

Figure 7-13. *Reducing the across clue*

One useful technique you can use is to write down the possible values for a set of cells. Figure 7-14 shows the possible values written for two sets of cells.

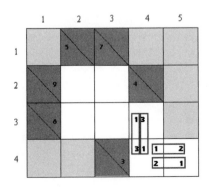

Figure 7-14. *Writing down the list of possible values for a set of cells*

Observe that the number 1 appears twice in cell (4,4). Because that is the only value that satisfies both the down clue (4) and across clue (3), you can now confirm cell (4,4) with the number 1.

Summary

In this chapter, you learned how to play the new Kakuro puzzle game. If you are coming from a Sudoku background, you should not find the puzzle too difficult. But most importantly, I hope you enjoy the games and have countless hours of fun and entertainment!

The SudokuPuzzle Class

Listing A-1 provides partial code for the SudokuPuzzle class that contains the logic to solve Sudoku puzzles (without the GUI code), as discussed throughout the book. The statements in bold indicate modified and newly added statements.

Listing A-1. *SudokuPuzzle Class Containing the Logic to Solve Sudoku Puzzles*

```
Public Class SudokuPuzzle
    '---used to represent the values in the grid---
    Private actual(9, 9) As Integer

    '---used to represent the possible values of cells in the grid---
    Private possible(9, 9) As String

    '---indicate if the brute-force subroutine should stop---
    Private BruteForceStop As Boolean = False

    '---used to store the state of the grid---
    Private ActualStack As New Stack(Of Integer(,))()
    Private PossibleStack As New Stack(Of String(,))()

    '---store the total score accumulated---
    Private totalscore As Integer

    '---back up a copy of the Actual array---
    Dim actual_backup(9, 9) As Integer

    '=================================================
    ' Steps to solve the puzzle
    '=================================================
    Private Function SolvePuzzle() As Boolean
        Dim changes As Boolean
        Dim ExitLoop As Boolean = False
```

```
Try
    Do '---Look for Triplets in Columns---
        Do '---Look for Triplets in Rows---
            Do '---Look for Triplets in Minigrids---
                Do '---Look for Twins in Columns---
                    Do '---Look for Twins in Rows---
                        Do '---Look for Twins in Minigrids---
                            Do '---Look for Lone Rangers in Columns---
                                Do '---Look for Lone Rangers in Rows---
                                    Do  '---Look for Lone Rangers in
                                    ' Minigrids---
                                        Do '---Perform Col/Row and Minigrid
                                        ' Elimination---
                                            changes = CheckColumnsAndRows()
                                            If IsPuzzleSolved() Then
                                                ExitLoop = True
                                                Exit Do
                                            End If
                                        Loop Until Not changes

                                        If ExitLoop Then Exit Do
                                        '---Look for Lone Rangers in
                                        ' Minigrids---
                                        changes = _
                                            LookForLoneRangersinMinigrids()
                                            If IsPuzzleSolved() Then
                                                ExitLoop = True
                                                Exit Do
                                            End If
                                    Loop Until Not changes

                                    If ExitLoop Then Exit Do
                                    '---Look for Lone Rangers in Rows---
                                    changes = LookForLoneRangersinRows()
                                        If IsPuzzleSolved() Then
                                            ExitLoop = True
                                            Exit Do
                                        End If
                                Loop Until Not changes
```

```
                If ExitLoop Then Exit Do
                '---Look for Lone Rangers in Columns---
                changes = LookForLoneRangersinColumns()
                 If IsPuzzleSolved() Then
                    ExitLoop = True
                    Exit Do
                End If
            Loop Until Not changes

            If ExitLoop Then Exit Do
            '---Look for Twins in Minigrids---
            changes = LookForTwinsinMinigrids()
             If IsPuzzleSolved() Then
                ExitLoop = True
                Exit Do
            End If
        Loop Until Not changes

        If ExitLoop Then Exit Do
        '---Look for Twins in Rows---
        changes = LookForTwinsinRows()
         If IsPuzzleSolved() Then
            ExitLoop = True
            Exit Do
        End If
    Loop Until Not changes

    If ExitLoop Then Exit Do
    '---Look for Twins in Columns---
    changes = LookForTwinsinColumns()
     If IsPuzzleSolved() Then
        ExitLoop = True
        Exit Do
    End If
Loop Until Not changes

If ExitLoop Then Exit Do
'---Look for Triplets in Minigrids---
changes = LookForTripletsinMinigrids()
```

```
            If IsPuzzleSolved() Then
                ExitLoop = True
                Exit Do
            End If
        Loop Until Not changes

        If ExitLoop Then Exit Do
        '---Look for Triplets in Rows---
        changes = LookForTripletsinRows()
         If IsPuzzleSolved() Then
            ExitLoop = True
            Exit Do
        End If
    Loop Until Not changes

    If ExitLoop Then Exit Do
    '---Look for Triplets in Columns---
    changes = LookForTripletsinColumns()
     If IsPuzzleSolved() Then
        ExitLoop = True
        Exit Do
    End If
Loop Until Not changes

Catch ex As Exception
    Throw New Exception("Invalid Move")
End Try

If IsPuzzleSolved() Then
    Return True
Else
    Return False
End If
End Function


'===================================================
' Calculates the possible values for all the cells
'===================================================
Private Function CheckColumnsAndRows() As Boolean
    Dim changes As Boolean = False
    '---check all cells---
    For row As Integer = 1 To 9
```

```vbnet
        For col As Integer = 1 To 9
            If actual(col, row) = 0 Then
                Try
                    possible(col, row) = CalculatePossibleValues(col, row)
                Catch ex As Exception
                    Throw New Exception("Invalid Move")
                End Try

                If possible(col, row).Length = 1 Then

                    '---number is confirmed---
                    actual(col, row) = CInt(possible(col, row))
                    changes = True

                    '---accumulate the total score---
                    totalscore += 1
                End If
            End If
        Next
    Next
    Return changes
End Function


'==================================================
' Calculates the possible values for a cell
'==================================================
Private Function CalculatePossibleValues( _
                ByVal col As Integer, _
                ByVal row As Integer) _
                As String
    Dim str As String
    If possible(col, row) = String.Empty Then
        str = "123456789"
    Else
        str = possible(col, row)
    End If

    Dim r, c As Integer
```

```vb
        '---Step (1) check by column---
        For r = 1 To 9
            If actual(col, r) <> 0 Then
                '---that means there is an actual value in it---
                str = str.Replace(actual(col, r).ToString(), String.Empty)
            End If
        Next

        '---Step (2) check by row---
        For c = 1 To 9
            If actual(c, row) <> 0 Then
                '---that means there is an actual value in it---
                str = str.Replace(actual(c, row).ToString(), String.Empty)
            End If
        Next

        '---Step (3) check within the minigrid---
        Dim startC, startR As Integer
        startC = col - ((col - 1) Mod 3)
        startR = row - ((row - 1) Mod 3)
        For rr As Integer = startR To startR + 2
            For cc As Integer = startC To startC + 2
                If actual(cc, rr) <> 0 Then
                    str = str.Replace(actual(cc, rr).ToString(), String.Empty)
                End If
            Next
        Next

        '---if possible value is string.Empty, then error---
        If str = String.Empty Then
            Throw New Exception("Invalid Move")
        End If
        Return str
    End Function


    '==================================================
    ' Look for Lone Rangers in Minigrids
    '==================================================
    Private Function LookForLoneRangersinMinigrids() As Boolean
        Dim changes As Boolean = False
        Dim NextMiniGrid As Boolean
        Dim occurrence As Integer
```

```vbnet
    Dim cPos, rPos As Integer

    '---check for each number from 1 to 9---
    For n As Integer = 1 To 9

        '---check the 9 minigrids---
        For r As Integer = 1 To 9 Step 3
            For c As Integer = 1 To 9 Step 3
                NextMiniGrid = False

                '---check within the minigrid---
                occurrence = 0
                For rr As Integer = 0 To 2
                    For cc As Integer = 0 To 2
                        If actual(c + cc, r + rr) = 0 AndAlso _
                            possible(c + cc, r + rr).Contains( _
                            n.ToString()) Then
                            occurrence += 1
                            cPos = c + cc
                            rPos = r + rr
                            If occurrence > 1 Then
                                NextMiniGrid = True
                                Exit For
                            End If
                        End If
                    Next
                    If NextMiniGrid Then Exit For
                Next

                If (Not NextMiniGrid) AndAlso occurrence = 1 Then
                    '---that means number is confirmed---
                    actual(cPos, rPos) = n
                    changes = True
                    '---accumulate the total score---
                    totalscore += 2
                End If
            Next
        Next
    Next
    Return changes
End Function
```

```vbnet
'============================================================
'Look for Lone Rangers in Rows
'============================================================
Private Function LookForLoneRangersinRows() As Boolean
    Dim changes As Boolean = False
    Dim occurrence As Integer
    Dim cPos, rPos As Integer

    '---check by row----
    For r As Integer = 1 To 9
        For n As Integer = 1 To 9
            occurrence = 0
            For c As Integer = 1 To 9
                If actual(c, r) = 0 AndAlso _
                    possible(c, r).Contains(n.ToString()) Then
                    occurrence += 1

                    '---if multiple occurrences, not a lone ranger anymore---
                    If occurrence > 1 Then Exit For
                    cPos = c
                    rPos = r
                End If
            Next
            If occurrence = 1 Then
                '--number is confirmed---
                actual(cPos, rPos) = n
                changes = True

                '---accumulate the total score---
                totalscore += 2
            End If
        Next
    Next
    Return changes
End Function


'============================================================
'Look for Lone Rangers in Columns
'============================================================
Private Function LookForLoneRangersinColumns() As Boolean
    Dim changes As Boolean = False
    Dim occurrence As Integer
```

```
        Dim cPos, rPos As Integer

    '----check by column----
    For c As Integer = 1 To 9
        For n As Integer = 1 To 9
            occurrence = 0
            For r As Integer = 1 To 9
                If actual(c, r) = 0 AndAlso _
                    possible(c, r).Contains(n.ToString()) Then
                    occurrence += 1

                    '---if multiple occurrences, not a lone ranger anymore---
                    If occurrence > 1 Then Exit For
                    cPos = c
                    rPos = r
                End If
            Next
            If occurrence = 1 Then
                '---number is confirmed---
                actual(cPos, rPos) = n
                changes = True

                '---accumulate the total score---
                totalscore += 2
            End If
        Next
    Next
    Return changes
End Function


'==================================================
' Look for Twins in Minigrids
'==================================================
Private Function LookForTwinsinMinigrids() As Boolean
    Dim changes As Boolean = False

    '---look for twins in each cell---
    For r As Integer = 1 To 9
        For c As Integer = 1 To 9
```

```vbnet
'---if two possible values, check for twins---
If actual(c, r) = 0 AndAlso possible(c, r).Length = 2 Then

    '---scan by the minigrid that the current cell is in---
    Dim startC, startR As Integer
    startC = c - ((c - 1) Mod 3)
    startR = r - ((r - 1) Mod 3)
    For rr As Integer = startR To startR + 2
        For cc As Integer = startC To startC + 2

            '---for cells other than the pair of twins---
            If (Not ((cc = c) AndAlso (rr = r))) AndAlso _
                possible(cc, rr) = possible(c, r) Then

                '---remove the twins from all the other possible
                ' values in the minigrid---
                For rrr As Integer = startR To startR + 2
                    For ccc As Integer = startC To startC + 2
                        If actual(ccc, rrr) = 0 AndAlso _
                            possible(ccc, rrr) <> _
                            possible(c, r) Then

                            '---save a copy of the original
                            ' possible values (twins)---
                            Dim original_possible As String = _
                                possible(ccc, rrr)

                            '---remove first twin number from
                            ' possible values---
                            possible(ccc, rrr) = _
                                possible(ccc, rrr).Replace( _
                                possible(c, r)(0), String.Empty)

                            '---remove second twin number from
                            ' possible values---
                            possible(ccc, rrr) = _
                                possible(ccc, rrr).Replace( _
                                possible(c, r)(1), String.Empty)
```

```vb
                                            '---if the possible values are
                                            ' modified, then set the changes
                                            ' variable to true to indicate
                                            ' that the possible values of cells
                                            ' in the minigrid have been modified---
                                            If original_possible <> _
                                                possible(ccc, rrr) Then
                                                    changes = True
                                            End If

                                            '---if possible value reduces to
                                            ' empty string, then the user has
                                            ' placed a move that results in
                                            ' the puzzle being not solvable---
                                            If possible(ccc, rrr) = _
                                                String.Empty Then
                                                    Throw New Exception("Invalid Move")
                                            End If

                                            '---if left with 1 possible value
                                            ' for the current cell, cell is
                                            ' confirmed---
                                            If possible(ccc, rrr).Length = 1 Then
                                                    actual(ccc, rrr) = _
                                                        CInt(possible(ccc, rrr))

                                                    '---accumulate the total score--
                                                    totalscore += 3
                                            End If
                                        End If
                                    Next
                                Next
                            End If
                        Next
                    Next
                End If
            Next
        Next
        Return changes
End Function
```

```vb
'======================================================
' Look for Twins in Rows
'======================================================
Private Function LookForTwinsinRows() As Boolean
    Dim changes As Boolean = False

    '---for each row, check each column in the row---
    For r As Integer = 1 To 9
        For c As Integer = 1 To 9

            '---if two possible values, check for twins---
            If actual(c, r) = 0 AndAlso possible(c, r).Length = 2 Then

                '--scan columns in this row---
                For cc As Integer = c + 1 To 9
                    If (possible(cc, r) = possible(c, r)) Then

                        '---remove the twins from all the other possible
                        ' values in the row---
                        For ccc As Integer = 1 To 9
                            If (actual(ccc, r) = 0) AndAlso _
                                (ccc <> c) AndAlso (ccc <> cc) Then

                                '---save a copy of the original possible
                                ' values (twins)---
                                Dim original_possible As String = _
                                    possible(ccc, r)

                                '---remove first twin number from possible
                                ' values---
                                possible(ccc, r) = possible(ccc, r).Replace( _
                                    possible(c, r)(0), String.Empty)

                                '---remove second twin number from possible
                                ' values---
                                possible(ccc, r) = possible(ccc, r).Replace( _
                                    possible(c, r)(1), String.Empty)

                                '---if the possible values are modified, then
                                ' set the changes variable to true to indicate
                                ' that the possible values of cells in the
                                ' minigrid have been modified---
```

```vbnet
                            If original_possible <> possible(ccc, r) Then
                                changes = True
                            End If

                            '---if possible value reduces to empty string,
                            ' then the user has placed a move that results
                            ' in the puzzle being not solvable---
                            If possible(ccc, r) = String.Empty Then
                                Throw New Exception("Invalid Move")
                            End If

                            '---if left with 1 possible value for the
                            ' current cell, cell is confirmed---
                            If possible(ccc, r).Length = 1 Then
                                actual(ccc, r) = CInt(possible(ccc, r))

                                '---accumulate the total score---
                                totalscore += 3
                            End If
                        End If
                    Next
                End If
            Next
        End If
    Next
    Next
    Return changes
End Function


'=====================================================
' Look for Twins in Columns
'=====================================================
Private Function LookForTwinsinColumns() As Boolean
    Dim changes As Boolean = False

    '---for each column, check each row in the column---
    For c As Integer = 1 To 9
        For r As Integer = 1 To 9

            '---if two possible values, check for twins---
            If actual(c, r) = 0 AndAlso possible(c, r).Length = 2 Then
```

```vb
'--scan rows in this column---
For rr As Integer = r + 1 To 9
    If (possible(c, rr) = possible(c, r)) Then

        '---remove the twins from all the other possible
        ' values in the row---
        For rrr As Integer = 1 To 9
            If (actual(c, rrr) = 0) AndAlso _
                (rrr <> r) AndAlso (rrr <> rr) Then

                '---save a copy of the original possible
                ' values (twins)---
                Dim original_possible As String = _
                    possible(c, rrr)

                '---remove first twin number from possible
                ' values---
                possible(c, rrr) = possible(c, rrr).Replace( _
                    possible(c, r)(0), String.Empty)

                '---remove second twin number from possible
                ' values---
                possible(c, rrr) = possible(c, rrr).Replace( _
                    possible(c, r)(1), String.Empty)

                '---if the possible values are modified, then
                'set the changes variable to true to indicate
                ' that the possible values of cells in the
                ' minigrid have been modified---
                If original_possible <> possible(c, rrr) Then
                    changes = True
                End If

                '---if possible value reduces to empty string,
                ' then the user has placed a move that results
                ' in the puzzle being not solvable---
                If possible(c, rrr) = String.Empty Then
                    Throw New Exception("Invalid Move")
                End If
```

```vb
                        '---if left with 1 possible value for the
                        ' current cell, cell is confirmed---
                        If possible(c, rrr).Length = 1 Then
                                actual(c, rrr) = CInt(possible(c, rrr))

                                '---accumulate the total score---
                                totalscore += 3
                        End If
                    End If
                Next
            End If
        Next
        End If
    Next
    Next
    Return changes
End Function


'====================================================
' Look for Triplets in Minigrids
'====================================================
Private Function LookForTripletsinMinigrids() As Boolean
    Dim changes As Boolean = False

    '---check each cell---
    For r As Integer = 1 To 9
        For c As Integer = 1 To 9

            '--- three possible values; check for triplets---
            If actual(c, r) = 0 AndAlso possible(c, r).Length = 3 Then

                '---first potential triplet found---
                Dim tripletsLocation As String = c.ToString() & r.ToString()

                '---scan by minigrid---
                Dim startC, startR As Integer
                startC = c - ((c - 1) Mod 3)
                startR = r - ((r - 1) Mod 3)
                For rr As Integer = startR To startR + 2
                    For cc As Integer = startC To startC + 2
```

```vb
                 If (Not ((cc = c) AndAlso (rr = r))) AndAlso _
                    ((possible(cc, rr) = possible(c, r)) OrElse _
                    (possible(cc, rr).Length = 2 AndAlso _
                    possible(c, r).Contains( _
                        possible(cc, rr)(0).ToString()) AndAlso _
                    possible(c, r).Contains( _
                        possible(cc, rr)(1).ToString())))) Then

                    '---save the coordinates of the triplets
                    tripletsLocation &= cc.ToString() & rr.ToString()
                 End If
             Next
         Next

         '--found 3 cells as triplets; remove all from the other
         ' cells---
         If tripletsLocation.Length = 6 Then

             '---remove each cell's possible values containing the
             ' triplet---
             For rrr As Integer = startR To startR + 2
                 For ccc As Integer = startC To startC + 2

                     '---look for the cell that is not part of the
                     ' 3 cells found---
                     If actual(ccc, rrr) = 0 AndAlso _
                        ccc <> CInt(tripletsLocation(0).ToString()) _
                        AndAlso _
                        rrr <> CInt(tripletsLocation(1).ToString()) _
                        AndAlso _
                        ccc <> CInt(tripletsLocation(2).ToString()) _
                        AndAlso _
                        rrr <> CInt(tripletsLocation(3).ToString()) _
                        AndAlso _
                        ccc <> CInt(tripletsLocation(4).ToString()) _
                        AndAlso _
                        rrr <> CInt(tripletsLocation(5).ToString()) Then

                         '---save the original possible values---
                         Dim original_possible As String = _
                            possible(ccc, rrr)
```

```vb
'---remove first triplet number from possible
' values---
possible(ccc, rrr) = _
   possible(ccc, rrr).Replace( _
      possible(c, r)(0), String.Empty)


'---remove second triplet number from possible
' values---
possible(ccc, rrr) = _
   possible(ccc, rrr).Replace( _
      possible(c, r)(1), String.Empty)


'---remove third triplet number from possible
' values---
possible(ccc, rrr) = _
   possible(ccc, rrr).Replace( _
      possible(c, r)(2), String.Empty)


'---if the possible values are modified, then
' set the changes variable to true to indicate
' that the possible values of cells in the
' minigrid have been modified---
If original_possible <> possible(ccc, rrr) Then
    changes = True
End If


'---if possible value reduces to empty string,
' then the user has placed a move that results
' in the puzzle being not solvable---
If possible(ccc, rrr) = String.Empty Then
    Throw New Exception("Invalid Move")
End If


'---if left with 1 possible value for the
' current cell, cell is confirmed---
If possible(ccc, rrr).Length = 1 Then
    actual(ccc, rrr) = CInt(possible(ccc, rrr))

    '---accumulate the total score---
    totalscore += 4
End If
End If
```

```vbnet
                    Next
                  Next
                End If
              End If
          Next
        Next
        Return changes
End Function


'==================================================
' Look for Triplets in Rows
'==================================================
Private Function LookForTripletsinRows() As Boolean
    Dim changes As Boolean = False

    '---for each row, check each column in the row---
    For r As Integer = 1 To 9
        For c As Integer = 1 To 9

            '--- three possible values; check for triplets---
            If actual(c, r) = 0 AndAlso possible(c, r).Length = 3 Then

                '---first potential triplet found---
                Dim tripletsLocation As String = c.ToString() & r.ToString()

                '---scans columns in this row---
                For cc As Integer = 1 To 9

                    '---look for other triplets---
                    If (cc <> c) AndAlso _
                       ((possible(cc, r) = possible(c, r)) OrElse _
                        (possible(cc, r).Length = 2 AndAlso _
                         possible(c, r).Contains( _
                             possible(cc, r)(0).ToString()) AndAlso _
                         possible(c, r).Contains( _
                             possible(cc, r)(1).ToString()))) Then

                        '---save the coordinates of the triplet---
                        tripletsLocation &= cc.ToString() & r.ToString()
                    End If
                Next
```

```vb
'--found 3 cells as triplets; remove all from the other
' cells---
If tripletsLocation.Length = 6 Then

    '---remove each cell's possible values containing the
    ' triplet---
    For ccc As Integer = 1 To 9
        If actual(ccc, r) = 0 AndAlso _
            ccc <> CInt(tripletsLocation(0).ToString()) _
            AndAlso _
            ccc <> CInt(tripletsLocation(2).ToString()) _
            AndAlso _
            ccc <> CInt(tripletsLocation(4).ToString()) Then

            '---save the original possible values---
            Dim original_possible As String = possible(ccc, r)

            '---remove first triplet number from possible
            ' values---
            possible(ccc, r) = _
                possible(ccc, r).Replace( _
                    possible(c, r)(0), String.Empty)

            '---remove second triplet number from possible
            ' values---
            possible(ccc, r) = _
                possible(ccc, r).Replace( _
                    possible(c, r)(1), String.Empty)

            '---remove third triplet number from possible
            ' values---
            possible(ccc, r) = _
                possible(ccc, r).Replace( _
                    possible(c, r)(2), String.Empty)

            '---if the possible values are modified, then set
            ' the changes variable to true to indicate that
            ' the possible values of cells in the minigrid
            ' have been modified---
            If original_possible <> possible(ccc, r) Then
                changes = True
            End If
```

```vb
                                '---if possible value reduces to empty string,
                                ' then the user has placed a move that results
                                ' in the puzzle being not solvable---
                                If possible(ccc, r) = String.Empty Then
                                    Throw New Exception("Invalid Move")
                                End If

                                '---if left with 1 possible value for the current
                                ' cell, cell is confirmed---
                                If possible(ccc, r).Length = 1 Then
                                    actual(ccc, r) = CInt(possible(ccc, r))

                                    '---accumulate the total score---
                                    totalscore += 4
                                End If
                            End If
                        Next
                    End If
                End If
            Next
        Next
        Return changes
End Function


'===================================================
' Look for Triplets in Columns
'===================================================
Private Function LookForTripletsinColumns() As Boolean
    Dim changes As Boolean = False

    '---for each column, check each row in the column---
    For c As Integer = 1 To 9
        For r As Integer = 1 To 9

            '--- three possible values; check for triplets---
            If actual(c, r) = 0 AndAlso possible(c, r).Length = 3 Then

                '---first potential triplet found---
                Dim tripletsLocation As String = c.ToString() & r.ToString()
```

```
'---scans rows in this column---
For rr As Integer = 1 To 9
    If (rr <> r) AndAlso _
        ((possible(c, rr) = possible(c, r)) OrElse _
        (possible(c, rr).Length = 2 AndAlso _
        possible(c, r).Contains( _
            possible(c, rr)(0).ToString()) AndAlso _
        possible(c, r).Contains( _
            possible(c, rr)(1).ToString())))) Then

            '---save the coordinates of the triplet---
            tripletsLocation += c.ToString() & rr.ToString()
    End If
Next

'--found 3 cells as triplets; remove all from the other cells---
If tripletsLocation.Length = 6 Then

    '---remove each cell's possible values containing the
    ' triplet---
    For rrr As Integer = 1 To 9
        If actual(c, rrr) = 0 AndAlso _
            rrr <> CInt(tripletsLocation(1).ToString()) _
            AndAlso _
            rrr <> CInt(tripletsLocation(3).ToString()) _
            AndAlso _
            rrr <> CInt(tripletsLocation(5).ToString()) Then

            '---save the original possible values---
            Dim original_possible As String = possible(c, rrr)

            '---remove first triplet number from possible
            ' values---
            possible(c, rrr) = _
               possible(c, rrr).Replace( _
                  possible(c, r)(0), String.Empty)

            '---remove second triplet number from possible
            ' values---
            possible(c, rrr) = _
               possible(c, rrr).Replace( _
                  possible(c, r)(1), String.Empty)
```

```vbnet
                                    '---remove third triplet number from possible
                                    ' values---
                                    possible(c, rrr) = _
                                        possible(c, rrr).Replace( _
                                            possible(c, r)(2), String.Empty)

                                    '---if the possible values are modified, then set
                                    ' the changes variable to true to indicate that
                                    ' the possible values of cells in the minigrid
                                    ' have been modified---
                                    If original_possible <> possible(c, rrr) Then
                                        changes = True
                                    End If

                                    '---if possible value reduces to empty string,
                                    ' then the user has placed a move that results
                                    ' in the puzzle being not solvable---
                                    If possible(c, rrr) = String.Empty Then
                                        Throw New Exception("Invalid Move")
                                    End If

                                    '---if left with 1 possible value for the current
                                    ' cell, cell is confirmed---
                                    If possible(c, rrr).Length = 1 Then
                                        actual(c, rrr) = CInt(possible(c, rrr))

                                        '---accumulate the total score---
                                        totalscore += 4
                                    End If
                                End If
                            Next
                        End If
                    End If
                Next
            Next
            Return changes
        End Function
```

```vb
'============================================================
' Find the cell with the least number of possible values
'============================================================
Private Sub FindCellWithFewestPossibleValues( _
    ByRef col As Integer, ByRef row As Integer)
    Dim min As Integer = 10
    For r As Integer = 1 To 9
        For c As Integer = 1 To 9
            If actual(c, r) = 0 AndAlso possible(c, r).Length < min Then
                min = possible(c, r).Length
                col = c
                row = r
            End If
        Next
    Next
End Sub


'===================================================
' Solve puzzle by brute force
'===================================================
Private Sub SolvePuzzleByBruteForce()
    Dim c, r As Integer

    '---accumulate the total score---
    totalscore += 5

    '---find out which cell has the least number of possible values---
    FindCellWithFewestPossibleValues(c, r)

    '---get the possible values for the chosen cell---
    Dim possibleValues As String = possible(c, r)

    '---push the actual and possible stacks into the stack---
    ActualStack.Push(CType(actual.Clone(), Integer(,)))
    PossibleStack.Push(CType(possible.Clone(), String(,)))

    '---select one value and try---
    For i As Integer = 0 To possibleValues.Length - 1
        actual(c, r) = CInt(possibleValues(i).ToString())
```

```vbnet
            Try
                If SolvePuzzle() Then
                    '---if the puzzle is solved, the recursion can stop now---
                    BruteForceStop = True
                    Return
                Else
                    '---no problem with current selection, proceed with next
                    ' cell---
                    SolvePuzzleByBruteForce()
                    If BruteForceStop Then Return
                End If
            Catch ex As Exception
                '---accumulate the total score---
                totalscore += 5
                actual = ActualStack.Pop()
                possible = PossibleStack.Pop()
            End Try
        Next
    End Sub


    '=================================================
    ' Check if the puzzle is solved
    '=================================================
    Private Function IsPuzzleSolved() As Boolean
        Dim pattern As String
        Dim r, c As Integer

        '---check row by row---
        For r = 1 To 9
            pattern = "123456789"
            For c = 1 To 9
                pattern = pattern.Replace(actual(c, r).ToString(), String.Empty)
            Next
            If pattern.Length > 0 Then
                Return False
            End If
        Next
```

```vbnet
        '---check col by col---
        For c = 1 To 9
            pattern = "123456789"
            For r = 1 To 9
                pattern = pattern.Replace(actual(c, r).ToString(), String.Empty)
            Next
            If pattern.Length > 0 Then
                Return False
            End If
        Next

        '---check by minigrid---
        For c = 1 To 9 Step 3
            pattern = "123456789"
            For r = 1 To 9 Step 3
                For cc As Integer = 0 To 2
                    For rr As Integer = 0 To 2
                        pattern = pattern.Replace( _
                            actual(c + cc, r + rr).ToString(), String.Empty)
                    Next
                Next
            Next
            If pattern.Length > 0 Then
                Return False
            End If
        Next
        Return True
    End Function
End Class
```

Index

You Need the Companion eBook

Your purchase of this book entitles you to its companion eBook for only $10.

We believe this Apress title will prove so indispensable that you'll want to carry it with you everywhere, which is why we are offering the companion eBook for $10 to customers who purchase this book now. Convenient and fully searchable, the eBook version of any content-rich, page-heavy Apress book makes a valuable addition to your programming library. You can easily find, copy, and apply code—and then perform examples by quickly toggling between instructions and the application. Even simultaneously tackling a donut, diet soda, and complex code becomes simplified with hands-free eBooks!

Once you purchase this book, getting the $10 companion eBook is simple:

❶ Visit **www.apress.com/promo/tendollars/**.

❷ Complete a basic registration form to receive a randomly generated question about this title.

❸ Answer the question correctly in 60 seconds and you will receive a promotional code to redeem for the $10 eBook.

2560 Ninth Street • Suite 219 • Berkeley, CA 94710

PROFESSIONALS™

JOIN THE APRESS FORUMS AND BE PART OF OUR COMMUNITY. You'll find discussions that cover topics of interest to IT professionals, programmers, and enthusiasts just like you. If you post a query to one of our forums, you can expect that some of the best minds in the business—especially Apress authors, who all write with *The Expert's Voice*™—will chime in to help you. Why not aim to become one of our most valuable participants (MVPs) and win cool stuff? Here's a sampling of what you'll find:

DATABASES
Data drives everything.

Share information, exchange ideas, and discuss any database programming or administration issues.

INTERNET TECHNOLOGIES AND NETWORKING
Try living without plumbing (and eventually IPv6).

Talk about networking topics including protocols, design, administration, wireless, wired, storage, backup, certifications, trends, and new technologies.

JAVA
We've come a long way from the old Oak tree.

Hang out and discuss Java in whatever flavor you choose: J2SE, J2EE, J2ME, Jakarta, and so on.

MAC OS X
All about the Zen of OS X.

OS X is both the present and the future for Mac apps. Make suggestions, offer up ideas, or boast about your new hardware.

OPEN SOURCE
Source code is good; understanding (open) source is better.

Discuss open source technologies and related topics such as PHP, MySQL, Linux, Perl, Apache, Python, and more.

PROGRAMMING/BUSINESS
Unfortunately, it is.

Talk about the Apress line of books that cover software methodology, best practices, and how programmers interact with the "suits."

WEB DEVELOPMENT/DESIGN
Ugly doesn't cut it anymore, and CGI is absurd.

Help is in sight for your site. Find design solutions for your projects and get ideas for building an interactive Web site.

SECURITY
Lots of bad guys out there—the good guys need help.

Discuss computer and network security issues here. Just don't let anyone else know the answers!

TECHNOLOGY IN ACTION
Cool things. Fun things.

It's after hours. It's time to play. Whether you're into LEGO® MINDSTORMS™ or turning an old PC into a DVR, this is where technology turns into fun.

WINDOWS
No defenestration here.

Ask questions about all aspects of Windows programming, get help on Microsoft technologies covered in Apress books, or provide feedback on any Apress Windows book.

HOW TO PARTICIPATE:
Go to the Apress Forums site at **http://forums.apress.com/**.
Click the New User link.